Voices from the Field II

Reflections on Comprehensive Community Change

Anne C. Kubisch

Patricia Auspos

Prudence Brown

Robert Chaskin

Karen Fulbright-Anderson

Ralph Hamilton

To purchase additional copies of this report, please contact:

The Aspen Institute
Fulfillment Office
P.O. Box 222
109 Houghton Lab Lane
Queenstown, MD 21658
Phone: (410) 820-5338
Fax: (410) 827-9174
E-mail: publications@aspeninstitute.org

CONTENTS

ACKNOWLEDGEMENTS

A LTHOUGH 10 PEOPLE LED THE PROCESS FOR REACHING THE conclusions presented here, in many ways it was the 63 people who participated in our interviews and meetings who "wrote" this book. (See Appendix II for a list of participants.) We are grateful to them for sharing their time and wisdom and hope that they find their voices represented in this final product.

Support from the following philanthropies made this project possible: The Annie E. Casey Foundation, The Edna McConnell Clark Foundation, Ford Foundation, The William and Flora Hewlett Foundation, W. K. Kellogg Foundation, The Robert Wood Johnson Foundation, The John D. and Catherine T. MacArthur Foundation, The David and Lucile Packard Foundation, and The Rockefeller Foundation. We are grateful for their financial and intellectual support of all of our work.

Editor Leila Fiester helped weave our ideas together and make them clear to many types of readers. Thebe Street Works in Minneapolis created the design and layout.

Finally, the Aspen Roundtable staff benefit from incredible leadership and support. The Co-chairs of the Roundtable—Harold

Richman and Lisbeth Schorr—provide inspiration, wisdom, and oversight to all of the staff's activities. The Roundtable's Administrative Assistant, Ivett Colon, ensured that all of the pieces of this complicated project actually worked. We are fortunate to have the three of them as colleagues.

ABOUT THE AUTHORS

T HIS BOOK IS THE PRODUCT OF COLLABORATION BETWEEN THE Roundtable on Comprehensive Community Initiatives of the Aspen Institute and the Chapin Hall Center for Children at the University of Chicago. A 10-member team defined the scope of work, conducted interviews, facilitated meetings, reviewed other research on relevant topics, analyzed the information, and identified the key messages to present. The team, with authors indicated by an asterisk, included:

- ❖ Andrea Anderson, Aspen Roundtable

- ❖ Patricia Auspos, Aspen Roundtable*

- ❖ Prudence Brown, Chapin Hall*

- ❖ Robert Chaskin, Chapin Hall*

- ❖ Karen Fulbright-Anderson, Aspen Roundtable*

- ❖ Ralph Hamilton, Chapin Hall*

❖ Anne Kubisch, Aspen Roundtable*

❖ Harold Richman, Chapin Hall and Co-chair of the Aspen Roundtable

❖ Lisbeth Schorr, Co-chair of the Aspen Roundtable

❖ Khatib Waheed, Aspen Roundtable

The Aspen Roundtable is a forum in which people affiliated with current community-change efforts meet to share the experiences, lessons, and problems of their work. (See Appendix I for a list of Roundtable members.) The Roundtable publishes and disseminates information about progress, challenges, and trends in the field of social and community change, and this book is part of that effort. The Roundtable's other work includes a project on how to evaluate, measure, and learn from community change efforts and a project to increase understanding of the ways in which structural racism affects poor communities and their prospects for revitalization. For more information about the Roundtable and its publications, see www.aspenroundtable.org.

The Chapin Hall Center for Children at the University of Chicago is a research and development center focusing on policies, practices, and programs affecting children and the families and communities in which they live. Chapin Hall provides research and technical assistance to federal, state, and municipal governments on a spectrum of issues including service system use, performance-based contracting, and measurement of child well-being. With both public and private support, Chapin Hall examines, evaluates, and documents public institutions and private initiatives that seek to support child and youth development and build the capacity of neighborhoods, community organizations, schools, and families to care for their children. For more information about Chapin Hall, see www.chapin.uchicago.edu.

INTRODUCTION

I N THE LATE 1980S, A NEW GENERATION OF COMMUNITY-BASED
anti-poverty ventures began. These efforts, which incorporated
lessons learned from 30 years of public-sector and philanthropic
investment in social change, became known as comprehensive community initiatives (CCIs).

CCIs typically are multi-year enterprises located in poor, urban
communities where physical and economic decline, social isolation,
and political disempowerment are the norm. Their leaders and participants have sought to improve neighborhood conditions and the
well-being of individuals and families by applying two principles:

❖ *Comprehensiveness*—an attempt to maximize the likelihood of
achieving positive results by simultaneously addressing the social,
economic, and physical conditions of a neighborhood; and

❖ *Community building*—an emphasis on participatory processes
that develop leadership, enhance "social capital" and personal
networks, and strengthen a community's capacity for improvement.

In 1997, the Aspen Roundtable on Comprehensive Community Initiatives distilled early lessons and emerging conclusions from the practices of CCIs during their first years. Drawing on information gleaned from focus groups with 94 different stakeholders—residents, program directors, funders, technical assistance providers, and evaluators—*Voices from the Field: Learning from the Early Work of Comprehensive Community Initiatives* described the overall functioning of CCIs and highlighted the fundamental challenges in their design and implementation. That volume (hereafter referred to as *Voices from the Field I*) was intended to synthesize then-current thinking and provoke useful discussion about the goals, approaches, and dynamics of community change.

Now, five years later, we can begin to weave the ongoing experience of CCIs into the fabric of knowledge about community change that comes from a broad array of initiatives, approaches, and activities—efforts that are all in some way about "community building" and "comprehensive community improvement." Together, these constitute a loosely defined, informal field of work, with some shared goals for community change and some common principles that guide action. The threads represented by CCIs offer lessons that reinforce, modify, and add to the experiences of other approaches. Collectively, they can increase our knowledge base about what it takes to substantially improve struggling neighborhoods and the quality of life within them. With this volume, we review the current state of these community-change efforts, synthesize what we know about their potential and their limitations, extract lessons about effective strategies, and propose a framework to guide future action.

As with *Voices from the Field I*, we began with practitioners' perspectives, derived from interviews and two interactive meetings of 63 people—drawn, once again, from a cross-section of key stakeholders in community change but representing a wider range of organizations, including CCIs, service organizations, community development corporations (CDCs), Empowerment Zones, philanthropies, and government agencies. Their comments and stories suggested the major themes and lessons for this book, and all of the quotations that follow (unless otherwise noted) come from those sources.

Recognizing that the supply of written materials about community change has become much richer in the years since *Voices from the Field I* was published, the authors of this book also incorporated findings from evaluations, academic research, and program documentation that clarify, support, or, in some cases, challenge the participants' comments. (For readers who want to delve more deeply into the issues and lessons, we present a set of recommended sources for further reading, listed at the end of the book by topic.)

The conclusions about place-based, anti-poverty work presented here are drawn both from the field's last 40 years of evolution and its current form of comprehensive, community-building approaches to neighborhood change. Our conclusions summarize the state of the field and where it should go; they are not intended as a rigid set of truths about designing and implementing these complex change efforts. Finally, it is important to note that the authors' own perspectives have inevitably shaped the way we present our sources' views.

THE MESSAGE OF THIS BOOK

The concept of "community" continues to be a powerful one around which to organize social policies and anti-poverty programs. Community is widely accepted as a launching pad for change for a variety of reasons—geographic, political, administrative, institutional, social, cultural, and even psychological and emotional. But the means for solving poor neighborhoods' problems lie only partially within communities' boundaries, and expectations for the outcomes of community-based change must reflect that reality.

Opportunities for significant improvement in disadvantaged neighborhoods therefore rely on two essential factors. The first is that communities must maximize their ability to produce whatever kinds of change are *within their control*. Effective local anti-poverty work thus requires enormous community "capacity"—a resource whose scarcity in impoverished neighborhoods debilitates and undermines much good work. To advance this agenda, we must improve our definition and understanding of community capacity and develop, test, evaluate, and reproduce strategies for building such internal strength.

The second essential factor is that communities must be able to use interactions with structures, resources, and other influences *beyond their boundaries* to the maximum advantage of the community. This means that community-change efforts must develop more sophisticated analyses of political, economic, and social dynamics and find better ways to tap into them, benefit from them, make demands on them, and improve their operations in distressed communities.

The challenge of committing to "community" while also recognizing its limitations has been a major struggle for CCIs and other community-change efforts. In the recent experience of CCIs, the challenge of tackling internal and external problems simultaneously has been so overwhelming that many confined themselves to what was possible: they focused almost exclusively on localized needs and did not address the major structural and institutional barriers that constrained their communities' ability to change. Now, some are re-examining and questioning the underlying premises of their work. As one leader asked, "What is it, exactly, that we think we are trying to do? Are we trying to alleviate poverty, or are we trying to make it 'less devastating' for those who live in it?"

These dilemmas have yet to be resolved, and they reflect the core of our message about the current "state of the field." Identifying the quandaries helps us to see that the community-change field has not yet had a faithful or full test of the concepts of comprehensiveness and community building. That, in turn, may explain why so many recent efforts have not lived up to their promise of comprehensive neighborhood transformation. Naming the problems is also the first step in developing a framework for how to proceed from here.

How should we act on this message? Unfortunately, the answer is not an easy one. The solution is not to abandon our current work but to do it better, with more sophistication and from a more strategic vantage point. It involves working more deeply within communities and more aggressively beyond their bounds. To do so, we need better theories of what the process of community change should really look like and better knowledge about how to do the work. Then, we will need to apply the theories and knowledge to a better infrastructure for action and sustained community improvement. We envision an *ecology of change* that has four principal levels:

❖ Change among community residents;

❖ Change within and among community-level institutions;

❖ Change among those who provide technical, financial, practical, and other supports; and

❖ Changes in broad policies and structures that have enormous influence on community residents and institutions.

Finally, we need to be sure to invest in a continuous cycle of tracking our work, distilling lessons, applying new information, and learning as we go. This book offers a first step in that direction.

MAKING THE CASE

This book builds its case by examining the experiences of CCIs and other community revitalization efforts within the context of a broader ecology of change. *Chapter I* presents a brief overview of "community" as an organizing concept and describes how CCIs evolved from a long history of comprehensive, community-driven approaches to social change. It summarizes the common characteristics, accomplishments, and limitations of CCIs and outlines the four-tiered ecology of community change in which CCIs and similar ventures operate.

CCIs explicitly identified the core principles of *comprehensiveness* and *community building* as an organizing framework for community change. An important lesson from much previous work had been that it unfolded in a piecemeal fashion: good programs for social services, economic development, and physical revitalization existed, but they were implemented in isolation from one another. The *comprehensiveness* theme of CCIs recognized that individual, family, and community circumstances were linked, and by linking our responses to those circumstances we could create a whole response that was more than the sum of its parts. The theme of *community building*, which responded to traditional top-down, externally driven anti-poverty efforts, recognized that neighborhoods contained their own capacities and relationships that could—and should—be mobilized. *Chapter II* examines those principles in depth and describes what people on the front lines of community change have learned about implementing them. It also suggests a number of reasons why the principles have not yet enabled community-change efforts to achieve their most ambitious goals.

Voices from the Field I described the complexity of the two core principles as the work of CCIs unfolded. The book identified two tensions embedded in the initiatives: the "process-product" tension and the "inside-outside" tension. The first highlighted the difficulty of producing outcomes in a timely way while simultaneously building capacity and respecting the community-building process. The second described the difficulty of negotiating roles and power dynamics for efforts that brought external resources into neighborhoods, especially when the goal was to empower residents and respect local conditions. In hindsight, identifying those tensions was the first step toward understanding the lessons contained in this book.

After a decade of experience, the record of CCIs is mixed. Many initiatives did indeed produce valuable change in their communities: they increased the quality and quantity of social services, economic activity, and physical improvements; they developed new capacities and relationships; and they brought new resources to the neighborhoods. But they were not the agents of community transformation that many hoped they would be. The neighborhoods in which they operate are still poor, and they still have critical socio-economic problems. In part, this is because the initiatives have not fully translated the principles of comprehensiveness and community building into action. It is also because the ways in which the core concepts were interpreted did not pay sufficient attention to the capacity needed within neighborhoods in order to implement a comprehensive community-building agenda. Nor was the need recognized for a sophisticated understanding of how to work with structures outside the community.

What, then, will it take to transform poor neighborhoods and the lives of their residents? The experiences outlined in Chapters I and II point to the importance of addressing the entire ecology of change. Each of the next four chapters examines a different level of that ecology: building capacity for change in individuals who live in communities, strengthening the capacities and connectedness of organizations and institutions within communities, using providers from outside the community to support change, and improving the policies and social structures that can influence neighborhood residents and institutions.

Chapter III focuses on individuals and the skills, knowledge, and opportunities they need to improve circumstances for themselves and their neighborhoods. It pays special attention to the benefits and challenges of three essential activities: developing local leadership, creating connections among community residents, and mobilizing people for action. *Chapter IV* takes a similar look at the capacities and connections that neighborhood institutions need to take on comprehensive community-building agendas. In particular, it explores issues and insights related to leadership, staffing, collaboration, governance, and racial and cultural issues.

Chapter V examines the issues faced by the people and organizations outside of communities who support local change efforts. It pursues four subjects that have great impact on the success of comprehensive community-building endeavors: funding levels, purposes, and relationships; access to technical assistance; evaluation and strategic data use; and opportunities for knowledge development.

Chapter VI examines implicit assumptions about how communities operate within the broader structures of society that influenced many recent community initiatives. Most notable is the emphasis on "local" work at the expense of attending to structural factors that exert enormous influence on poor communities. This problem has played out in the ways in which community-building efforts have (or have not) addressed the policies and practices of the public and private sectors. The message of Chapter VI is that the framework for confronting these dynamics has been weak or missing in many recent change efforts, and that framework must be reinvigorated so that the issues fall squarely on the agendas of community-change efforts. It calls for a careful consideration of what community efforts can do on their own and how they can build alliances with change agents who are better-positioned to affect the larger structural, institutional, and political issues.

The *Conclusion* suggests that, after 10 years of implementation, CCIs have generated valuable insights about how to improve poor communities—lessons that apply to all efforts to transform neighborhoods, not just CCIs—but, in the end, the approach still has much room for improvement. The enduring aspects of CCIs seem to be not the initiatives themselves but the capacity for change that they build, the connections they forge among people and organizations, the broad, strategic principles that they promote, and the opportunities for knowledge development that they provide. A better framework for community change would put those elements front and center.

I.

COMMUNITIES AND COMMUNITY CHANGE

THE IDEA OF COMMUNITY EVOKES POWERFUL IMAGES AND emotions. It suggests a sense of identity, belonging, shared circumstance, and common cause. Local, geographically defined communities have long provided a lever for social change. They not only form the bedrock of broader efforts to organize action, they also are a focus of change in themselves, especially when it comes to improving the lives of people in poverty.

This chapter describes how and why community-based approaches to change have become a significant part of the social policy landscape. It describes how the newest iteration of community-change approaches, comprehensive community initiatives (CCIs), evolved, and it summarizes their attributes and the accomplishments and limitations of the approach.

We explore two underlying themes here. The first is that CCIs are an important but still imperfect piece of the overall social change process. Their virtues and their flaws bear closer scrutiny in the search for effective ways to improve the well-being of the most disadvantaged members of society. Second, there is a broad ecology in which community change operates, and CCIs are only one of the elements.

WHY COMMUNITY?

For generations, the concept of community has shaped social policy and practice in the United States. For comprehensive community initiatives, the term "community" has several intertwined meanings. It is a place, usually a neighborhood or group of neighborhoods. The notion of "place" is important because communities provide infrastructure, facilities, goods, and services for their residents—or they don't, because the community is depleted. Either way, the community shapes its members' experiences and well-being. Community boundaries and circumstances also define political representation and administrative functioning.

Community means more than a defined geographic area and its institutions, however. Communities are an important source of cultural, social, and civic identity for many Americans. The collective values represented by "community" influence how residents interact with and influence one another in both positive and negative ways. They provide opportunities for individuals and their families to develop a sense of belonging and connection.

Communities are an important entry point for social change for three reasons: poverty and related social problems tend to be concentrated in certain neighborhoods; communities have effects on individual and family well-being, and those influences are amenable to change; and neighborhoods are basic units of social, economic, and political organization.

Poverty and related social problems tend to be concentrated in certain neighborhoods.

In the words of one practitioner,

> Poverty has become concentrated because of a lot of large forces; that process has brought about concentration of the poor, those who are less skilled and less connected to the labor force, which has led to isolation and has had behavioral implications. Therefore we need to address all of these issues.

Economic distress is strongly correlated with racial segregation, political disempowerment, and social problems. By and large, poor people are more bound to "place" than are their middle-class counterparts and they are isolated from sources of power and change.

Communities have effects on individual and family well-being, and those influences are amenable to change.

Although social bonds are less concentrated locally than at other times in our country's history, neighborhoods—poor and non-poor—continue to provide a foundation for social life. Relationships among neighborhood residents can provide important social, emotional, and psychological support. Local organizations and institutions can act as advocates for community needs or as conduits to other resources. Individuals (residents, shopkeepers, workers, service providers, property owners) respond to community circumstances, influence neighborhood dynamics, and form relationships that can facilitate or constrain access to information, assistance, opportunities, community empowerment, and collective action.

Communities also are the building blocks of civic and political life. The small scale of neighborhood life can foster face-to-face interaction and provide opportunities for residents to participate in decision making—elements of the civic process that are vital to American democracy.

This dimension of community occupies an important place in current community-building ventures. Although neighborhoods have changed over time, the vision of community as a place of belonging and solidarity remains powerful. At the same time, the view of community as the locus of intimate social ties is being appropriately challenged. Many people caution against idealizing the concept:

> *We still have this romance about neighborhoods, villages, knowing and loving neighborhoods. It assumes that the concept of neighborhood does not evolve, that neighborhoods must be as they used to be. . . . Working toward kumbayah is unrealistic. We can fall far short of that and still be very successful.*

Neighborhoods are basic units of social, economic, and political organization.

Small areas are manageable targets for change, administratively and financially. Resources for physical, social, and economic change can be concentrated in communities and, in theory, so can their effects. Thus, communities have long been and continue to be both a target of change and a launching pad for grassroots change.

THE EMERGENCE OF COMPREHENSIVE COMMUNITY INITIATIVES (CCIs)

The most recent phase of community-oriented change began toward the second half of the 20th century. It has many roots: the emphasis on racial justice and equity that came out of the civil rights movement; concern about the persistence of urban poverty; the emergence of the philanthropic sector; acceptance of the role of government as an agent of social change; a growing base of social science research on the nature of social problems; and the strength of neighborhood organizations. These influences converged to create an approach to change based on institutional reform, integration of programmatic strategies, and the joint participation of local leaders and low-income residents in planning and delivering services and development activities.

Leadership came from the philanthropic sector, especially the Ford Foundation's Gray Areas program, and the federal government, through its War on Poverty and Community Action Program. Over the years, they were joined by social service agencies, local coalitions, public/private partnerships, community organizing groups, progressive churches, and specially created local organizations such as community development corporations (CDCs).

Those actors established the central importance of citizen participation in neighborhood redevelopment. They created local planning, development, and service systems that continue today. They sparked the creation of an infrastructure for technical assistance, research and evaluation, and financing to support local work. And they advanced a generation of leaders who became influential figures in local government, private foundations, community organizing and development, and the nonprofit sector. Although they did not always live up to their mandate for broad community change, the anti-poverty initiatives of the last half of the 20th century did contribute to the elements that guide today's community-building and community-change efforts.

In the late 1980s, comprehensive community initiatives (CCIs) were created to bring together, borrow from, build on, and revisit the experiences and lessons of previous approaches to community change. They emerged in an era of new federalism, which emphasized individualism and self-help and signaled a general shrinking of the federal government's role. Most initiatives have been spearheaded by national, regional, or local foundations, although several public-sector initiatives have become an important part of the mix, notably the federal Empowerment Zone/Enterprise Community (EZ/EC) and HOPE VI initiatives. By the turn of the century, most major cities had a CCI in at least one neighborhood.

Like many of their predecessors, CCIs are based on two powerful concepts: they address community needs *comprehensively*, and they emphasize *community building* by strengthening individual, organizational, and community capacity. Although they vary from place to place, they generally have the following characteristics:

❖ *They are* initiatives *rather than projects or programs.* This means that CCIs have a prescribed beginning and end. Their funding lasts longer than a traditional grant (usually 5–10 years).

❖ *A funder's goals usually serve as the catalyst.* While this is not always the case, usually CCIs are instigated and sponsored by a funder or group of funders, and the sponsor often is very engaged throughout the initiative's duration.

❖ *They have an explicitly comprehensive approach.* CCIs operate on the premise that problems in poor communities have many interrelated causes and therefore their solutions must involve an integrated array of sectors and resources. They aim to foster synergistic interactions that produce greater or faster changes than narrower programs.

❖ *They promote deliberate, community-based planning, grounded in the history of the community and the interests of community residents.* Although CCIs have external sponsors, their plans usually are developed through an intentional local process that considers community needs, interests, assets, and resources. The aim is to produce a community-driven strategic plan that guides all major actions.

❖ *They rely on governance structures or collaborative partnerships within the community.* The entities that govern CCIs emphasize local oversight and accountability to the community. In some instances, CCIs are housed in existing neighborhood organizations. In other cases, CCIs create new entities to manage activities. Because they have multiple goals, CCIs often work to develop collaboration among a range of institutional players in the neighborhood.

❖ *They draw on an array of external organizations for technical assistance, research, and other supports.* The sponsors put local stakeholders in touch with outside experts who then provide "wrap-around" supports, often with independent funding from the sponsor.

❖ *They seek partnerships between the community and external sources of political and economic power.* CCIs try to stimulate collaboration between community and external stakeholder, across the public, private, and nonprofit sectors. They use this process to search for politically viable, broadly acceptable solutions and to attract new funds to the neighborhood. The CCI funder sometimes plays a role in leveraging other resources, in addition to providing financial assistance.

❖ *They have a learning component.* Most CCIs have an explicit learning function, and independent evaluations are usually funded by the sponsor.

CCIs approach community change as a complex process with many interacting elements. They are based on the theory that a critical set of experiences, capacities, ideas, and resources—both within and outside the neighborhood—can be melded into a package that triggers and sustains neighborhood transformation. In this case, the silver bullet is not a solitary thing or event but rather the highly strategic combination of people, programs, organizations, capacities, connections, technologies, politics, and funding streams. Initiative planners hope that this strategic realignment of elements, when combined with new and flexible CCI funding, will produce the changes that previously eluded community change agents. Moreover, they expect that the fresh resources CCIs bring to neighborhoods will attract continuing public and private investment, which will help sustain change over time.

ACCOMPLISHMENTS AND LIMITATIONS OF CCIs

The comprehensive community initiatives of the 1990s began with ambitious goals. Using time-limited funds, they expected to generate long-term improvements in highly distressed communities. They aimed to accomplish this by applying lessons from an array of successful economic, social, and physical revitalization programs and by experimenting with new ideas about fighting poverty.

What is their record so far? Reviews of CCI evaluations suggest that CCIs can claim three basic accomplishments in neighborhoods: increases in programs that strengthen infrastructure and services, increases in neighborhood capacity, and increases in resources flowing into the neighborhood.

Increases in programs that strengthen infrastructure and services

CCIs have produced tangible results by investing in a variety of programs. CCI-supported efforts to improve physical infrastructure have built or rehabilitated housing and contributed to the revitalization of commercial areas, parks, and other public spaces—popular improvements because they can inspire other kinds of investments. CCI investments in employment assistance and economic development programs have helped community residents gain job skills and enter the workforce, and they have spawned new commercial enterprises.

Programs to enhance the well-being of children and families have produced new neighborhood services that fill critical gaps, including health and mental health care, child care, and after-school care. The asset-oriented approach taken by CCIs has meant that many of these programs emphasize family support, crisis prevention, and developmental services. CCIs also have enhanced, expanded, or recast existing community services to reflect an emphasis on building community rather than just fixing problems.

A variety of CCI-sponsored programs that address the quality of life help to foster community identity and pride. These include formal and informal activities, such as local newspapers, community celebrations, recreational activities, graffiti paint-outs, and block watches.

Increases in the capacity of individuals and organizations

The focus on community building has led CCIs to promote resident leadership, primarily by involving community members in initiative planning and governance. Although the total number of active residents in any given neighborhood may be small, evaluations consistently suggest that residents who participate directly in CCIs gain new skills and experience in collective planning and decision making, participation on boards, speaking in public, and representing community interests.

The success of CCIs' attempts to build "social capital"—to reweave the social fabric of the neighborhood—is difficult to measure; evidence of such change is largely anecdotal. People working on the frontlines of CCIs report that residents have been mobilized to participate in community programs and civic activities in new ways, new relationships have formed among community members, and sources of support are enhanced.

CCI participants have invested considerable time and effort in strengthening key neighborhood organizations. Financial and technical assistance have helped community institutions develop capacities for community assessment, information management, community outreach, service integration, fundraising, and policy analysis. CCIs also have forged partnerships among organizations by bringing new local institutions to the table. Participants report that the number of opportunities for collaboration among organizations has grown.

Increases in resources

CCIs have brought new financial resources to their neighborhoods. Many have tapped new streams of state and local dollars in youth development, mental health services, child welfare and other domains. Many also have attracted private-sector investment for local business or housing development.

In sum, CCIs have augmented and expanded many good programs and practices. They also have developed new ways of doing business that lay the groundwork for ongoing change. New philanthropic and public initiatives, for example, now emphasize the importance of community context, resident participation and self-determination, integrated and holistic thinking, partnerships across stakeholder groups, and a developmental or asset focus. This is true not only for broad community revitalization efforts but also for targeted efforts, such as those designed to improve social services, increase employment, or reduce crime.

Despite their successes, however, CCIs have not been able to transform poor neighborhoods. Many practitioners of community change say that the challenge of pulling diverse stakeholders together in new ways, around a resident-driven agenda and nontraditional practices, was too great. CCIs aimed to encompass every element of significant neighborhood change—the people, the organizations, the programs, the supports, and the outside resources—but they did not have the capacity or resources to put all of the elements in place or ensure that they worked effectively.

Further, many observers point out that CCIs were implemented as though neighborhoods had the power to achieve significant change in spite of the rest of the world. As one analyst noted:

> *The danger . . . is the implicit assumption that communities which have been systematically exploited and neglected for generations, and isolated from lucrative job markets, public transportation networks, adequate education, and service systems, can nevertheless begin to revive themselves essentially by their own effort. Structural and institutional barriers that continue to block minority advancement can be overcome or made irrelevant, it is assumed, by denser collaborative networks.*

CCIs have ended up with a focus on treating manifestations of poverty that were caused by factors outside their purview, including deeply embedded racism, changes in the political and funding climates, population mobility, and public policies and investments that isolate poor people in the inner cities. (Those structural issues pervade the themes presented in this book, and they are discussed more in Chapters V and VI.) Even when CCI participants have wanted to address issues of power, racism, and economic inequality, they have lacked the funding or capacity to do so.

Practitioners and observers now suggest that CCIs promised too much and, consequently, are being judged by unrealistic standards. CCIs' ambitious goals have bumped up against the limitations of community-building practices, suggesting a need to understand and mobilize many more levels of change. That will require new analytical skills, capacities, and alliances, however—both within communities and with outside resources (see Chapters IV, V, and VI). Practitioners do not advocate abandoning a commitment to place, but they do call for a better understanding, at the local level, of what triggers change and how people can apply those levers individually and collectively.

THE ECOLOGY OF COMMUNITY CHANGE

The successes and disappointments of CCIs—especially when considered alongside the experiences of other community-change efforts over the years—lead us to re-examine what can be done to improve distressed communities, and how to do it best. The remainder of this book explores those topics. But first, it is worth thinking about who needs to be part of the community change process.

Experience suggests that a variety of individuals, organizations, and relationships contribute directly to community change, serve as assets or partners, and round out our understanding of what might be called the "ecology" of community change.[1] We recognize four levels of action, with participants playing different roles at each level.

The first level involves *residents*, both individuals and families. Although CCIs are community-level interventions and seek community-level outcomes, the principle of community building recognizes that residents are a neighborhood's most important resource. As such, CCIs seek to develop the skills residents need to lead the change process. CCIs also recognize that the connections among individuals are powerful assets for neighborhood change, both as sources of support and as instruments for collective action. Thus CCIs aim to strengthen those relationships.

The second level involves *ground-level actors*—community groups and organizations that carry out the day-to-day work of com-

---

[1]This discussion of the ecology of community change borrows heavily from the significant contribution made by Ferguson and Stoutland (1999) to our understanding of the "community development system."

munity revitalization. These participants are directly engaged in community-building activities; they connect stakeholders, build assets, employ residents, provide services, and mobilize action. Some concentrate on a particular function, such as advocacy, service delivery, or community organizing; some focus on a population, such as the young or elderly; and some target specific community assets, such as housing or jobs.

Most ground-level participants play several roles, overlapping with the work of other organizations and shifting their focus in response to community needs and opportunities. A community health provider, for example, may organize residents to advocate for better city sanitation services; a church may create a development group to provide low-income housing; a CDC may move beyond housing to provide social services or beyond services to coordinate resources on behalf of the community. Outside agents such as foundations and local governments often look to these organizations to lead planning efforts or act as intermediaries.

Much of the work of CCIs focuses on turning ground-level stakeholders into an infrastructure for civic capacity and broader neighborhood change—a structure that helps community members make plans and forge connections with city government, developers, and other allies outside the neighborhood. In the words of one CDC director,

> *We need to develop structure first—neighborhood associations,*
> *an assembly model—and use this power structure to communi-*
> *cate, identify issues, and mobilize resident strength.*

The third level involves *organizations that provide support*: funders, technical assistance providers, research and training institutions, and intermediaries. These entities may work within the community or beyond it. They may be catalysts for activity or contribute directly to change. They may convene or support ground-level organizations with money, information, connections, and influence. They may extend the work of ground-level organizations, develop them in new directions, or disseminate lessons and models of good practice. Many of these actors play numerous roles and, depending on circumstances, may work apart from, parallel to, or in connection with others in the neighborhood.

The fourth level involves *entities that focus on public- and private-sector policy issues, advocacy, and political change.* They may be grounded in community-level organizing, but they operate less as part of a support system for community building than as an autonomous force for change at broader levels of action. Although this fourth level can include both ground-level actors and support providers, the efforts of each participant may not be well coordinated. Community building at the neighborhood level rarely has links to broader social movements and policy advocacy at the state and national levels; the links that do exist tend to form around episodic policy initiatives. As a result, opportunities for community change sometimes fall through the cracks.

THE ARRAY OF PEOPLE AND ORGANIZATIONS THAT PARTICIPATE IN community change is extensive, and each actor's effectiveness depends on the capacity to plan and implement good strategies and the ability to forge alliances or other connections that promote change. Much of the discussion in the rest of this book focuses on ways to strengthen those capacities and connections. But there is another dimension that shapes capacities and connections: the core principles of *comprehensiveness* and *community building*, which many practitioners, residents, technical experts, researchers, and funders view as the fundamental basis of their work. Chapter II examines those principles and the assumptions behind them. It describes how the principles have been interpreted and put into practice, and it begins to reflect on how they have changed or held up over time.

II.

The Core Principles of Comprehensiveness and Community Building

For more than a decade, CCIs have assumed that the principles of comprehensive or holistic programming and community building can produce significant improvements in poor neighborhoods. Many people working to improve communities—including the residents, practitioners, funders, researchers, and technical experts interviewed for this report—continue to believe that these two principles signal important departures from traditional models for change that are more categorical, deficit-oriented, and disempowering.

But the core principles have not provided a clear enough roadmap for action, and the overall theory for how to use them to change poor neighborhoods has not been well articulated. What kinds of outcomes can and cannot be expected by working according to these principles? What do they look like in operation?

This chapter re-examines the principles of comprehensiveness and community building in light of CCIs' accomplishments. It identifies the aspects that are commonly accepted, those that require more prominence and investment, and those that should be redefined or de-emphasized. It summarizes how the meaning and use of the core concepts have changed, and it presents general insights for current and future community-change efforts.

PRINCIPLE ONE: COMPREHENSIVENESS

At the core of *comprehensiveness* is the idea that families and communities are complex systems, with many layers of relationships and interactions, and that they face multi-faceted, interconnected problems. Therefore, it takes an integrated effort operating on many fronts—economic, social, political, physical, and cultural—to fundamentally transform the conditions that shape the lives of children and families.

Although the term "comprehensiveness" has developed confusing and sometimes negative connotations, the view that a holistic and integrative approach should guide planning and action is widely held.

An important aim of a comprehensive approach is *synergy*—the assumption that if a community-change venture simultaneously operates a variety of programs addressing a range of issues, the combined results will produce larger impacts than the programs would have produced independently. The idea that elements of an initiative can be mutually reinforcing is a key premise of CCIs.

MODELS FOR COMPREHENSIVENESS

To understand different approaches to comprehensiveness, it helps to view CCIs in the context of the broader field of community change. Three basic approaches for planning and embarking on comprehensive change have emerged over the years: (1) mounting an initiative that is comprehensive from the outset, (2) using a "strategic driver" to focus the activities, and (3) starting with one type of program activity and adding others as the initiative or the organization matures. Initiatives have sometimes combined these models to address different needs at various stages of development.

Being comprehensive from the outset

Many of the classic CCIs established by foundations in the late 1980s and 1990s had a mandate from the outset to address the physical, economic, and social dimensions of neighborhood life comprehensively. These initiatives usually developed programs in at least three or four major areas such as education, employment, economic development, health, housing and physical infrastructure, and crime and safety. Some have attempted to address an even wider span of neighborhood conditions. Because these CCIs have relied on a large number of organizations to support and implement their neighborhood plans, they have typically used a collaborative structure for planning and management.

Organizing around a "strategic driver"

Instead of mounting an array of programs simultaneously, some CCIs have identified a single issue (or a few overarching issues) to be used as a driver or catalyst for determining target outcomes, program approaches, and activities. This tactic has enabled initiatives to be comprehensive in their analysis of issues and solutions while also focusing on well-defined goals in specific domains. Examples of strategic drivers include employment, housing, health, school readiness, crime reduction, and substance abuse.

Taking an organic, incremental approach

A third approach is to begin with a single focus or activity and incrementally expand into other program areas, moving gradually toward a comprehensive scope of work. CCIs that follow this strategy expand as they mature and develop experience and credibility. In most cases, the organization takes responsibility for implementing projects rather than simply managing, monitoring, or coordinating the work of other neighborhood groups.

There are several examples of mature organizations, including CDCs and service agencies, that now oversee a comprehensive array of programs and activities in specific neighborhoods. Their directors emphasize, however, that they did not start with the intention of being comprehensive but became more multi-faceted as needs arose.

OBSERVATIONS ABOUT COMPREHENSIVENESS

Leaders in the field of community change continue to underscore the importance of viewing communities as complex systems requiring comprehensive solutions. But the challenges associated with making comprehensiveness a reality have led practitioners, funders, evaluators, and other stakeholders to experiment with various ways of putting the concept into practice. That experience suggests the following observations.

Being comprehensive means viewing problems and solutions through a comprehensive lens and approaching the work strategically. It does not mean doing everything at once.

Many seasoned observers and funders of CCIs have moved away from the "comprehensive-at-the-outset" model described above. They now think that such initiatives dissipate energy and resources by trying to do too much or become paralyzed by the task. One evaluator warned, "Comprehensiveness is a recipe for confusion." Added a funder, "CCIs will drown under their own weight if they try to do everything simultaneously."

This lesson suggests that comprehensive change efforts should cut through the range of available options and select those that are most appropriate and viable. The challenge here is to avoid getting so involved in the conduct of one or more programs that participants get distracted from the broader agenda. It is possible to do many diverse things and still maintain a sense of coherence about overall goals, but such efforts require solid plans, the resources to execute them, and constant reassessment of the link between daily activities and long-term goals.

Comprehensiveness should evolve along with the capacity to implement change.

Some CCI practitioners believe that building incrementally from a modest but firm foundation, as experience and capacity increase, produces stronger and longer-lasting results. Trying to do too many things at once can strain program operations, spread resources too thinly, and push

> "It's better to create a large footprint for building and add to it as you go along rather than construct the whole thing up front."
>
> —CCI funder

initiatives to act before their participants have sufficient skills, knowledge, or credibility. As one technical assistance provider noted,

> *The most successful examples got to be comprehensive by accretion—by being strategic over time, entrepreneurial. If they try to be comprehensive from the beginning, organizations are likely to get stuck.*

Practitioners recommend beginning with projects that show tangible, short-term results but still keep the broader vision in mind. That approach gives the people responsible for implementing the plan a chance to see what works and what doesn't. Short-term results also motivate potential allies to come on board.

The downside of this approach is that the developmental process may be slow or remain narrowly focused. The aim of concentrating resources and expertise in the context of community change initiatives is, after all, to improve neighborhood-wide conditions for individuals and families as quickly as possible.

Does accepting an "organic" process mean it is not possible to stimulate faster change? Several funders and intermediaries are responding to this question by testing how well the strategic driver model can help initiatives focus their energies, prioritize actions, develop plans, and integrate diverse projects while also remaining flexible and comprehensive. They suggest that the strategic driver should be (1) consistent with the community's interests and (2) capable of inspiring support and investment. "Start where people have the most need or interest," one funder advised. "The work has to be done strategically, like the starting brick in building a house," another funder observed. "There has to be something that can have success and garner resources."

Aiming for comprehensiveness means deliberately making connections across all aspects of the work and looking for opportunities to create synergy.

The comprehensive lens encourages people to form links among all components of an initiative. This can happen horizontally across programs or vertically across levels of participants. In the former case, there is a long tradition of making connections *within* sectors of work, such as integrated social services. But a growing number of program experiments also links *across* sectors—between housing construction and youth development, for example, or between environmental clean-up and workforce development.

Vertical linkages are much more of a challenge. They are especially hard to create between grassroots entities and municipal, regional, or national change agents. A prominent theme of this book is that CCIs, for the most part, have been unable to develop powerful strategies for making vertical linkages or for forging partnerships with change agents beyond the community. Some observers suggest that it should not be the responsibility of community-level actors to promote broad institutional or policy changes—that it simply is not their strength. Others argue that if community-change ventures don't pay attention to these issues they will be "destined to just play in the sandbox," as one expert put it.

Links among programs, while important, do not necessarily constitute a comprehensive change agenda. Experience shows it is easier to figure out the mechanics of linking program elements than to maintain a sense of how various pieces can integrate, interact, and produce a whole that is more than the sum of its parts. Synergy has been an elusive goal for CCIs

PRINCIPLE TWO: COMMUNITY BUILDING

Community building—the process of strengthening the ability of neighborhood residents, organizations, and institutions to foster and sustain neighborhood change, both individually and collectively—is vital to the work of CCIs and many other community-change efforts. The belief that community residents can be agents of change, rather than just beneficiaries or clients, is probably the quality that most distinguishes community building from traditional programs and activities.

Practitioners believe that community building is a democratic process and that the people who are most affected by what happens in a community have the right to be included in discussions and decisions about what and how things should be done. This dimension of the work often is what truly motivates leaders, staff, and residents as they carry out their daily activities. It underscores the values of equity, self-determination, social justice, and respect for diversity that they believe are fundamental to healthy communities.

The community-building principle also recognizes that strong communities are built on the strengths of their residents and the relationships among them. The isolation of poor neighborhoods can undermine residents' emotional, psychological, and social supports and sap the energy and the will they need to produce changes. Community building tries to weave or repair the social fabric of a neighborhood by expanding and strengthening informal ties among residents. It also aims to link community members with supportive individuals, organizations, and resources outside the neighborhood.

Community building, as the name suggests, is an ongoing process. In the words of one funder, "Is there such a thing as a 'built' community? I don't think so. There's always room for improvement." The goal is to put in place the will, resources, and capacity needed to sustain local improvement beyond the life of an initiative.

MODELS FOR COMMUNITY BUILDING

Although successful CDCs and other community-based organizations began putting the philosophy into practice well before it went by the name "community building," CCIs played a pivotal role in placing the principle front and center, backing it with financial and technical resources, finding ways to implement it, and attempting to measure it. Community building's position within recent community-change initiatives spans the spectrum from being a means to an end to being the end itself.

Community building as a means to an end

Some CCIs undertake community building as a means for reaching or enhancing programmatic goals (e.g., increasing employment, building better housing, improving health outcomes). From the perspective of these practitioners, community building is one of many instruments for change—something that occurs in the service of the initiative. According to one CCI director,

> *Community building must be done around real projects designed to revitalize the neighborhood in response to the needs and issues articulated by the community. It's not just a matter of holding meetings. It must be outcomes oriented. . . . it must be intertwined with programs. It's not an approach by itself: it feeds on and is fed by outcome-oriented projects.*

Advocates of this view are sometimes impatient with the process-oriented, "touchy-feely" community builders who, they believe, are lax about linking the work to outcomes. As a representative from one neighborhood-based employment effort explained, "If we find out that the neighborhood residents didn't get jobs, we will not have succeeded. If we find out that they increased their self-esteem but didn't get jobs, we just won't accept that."

Community building as an end in itself

Other practitioners believe that community building is an end in itself, a goal to pursue. Their initiatives use community building to drive all strategic decisions, and they assume that community-building outcomes—resident leadership, social capital, and neighborhood empowerment—are both valuable in their own right and essential for producing other types of change. People who subscribe to this view would argue that a community improvement effort that builds housing or increases employment but does not engage or empower residents is not successful.

OBSERVATIONS ABOUT COMMUNITY BUILDING

The practitioners and stakeholders interviewed for this book identified the following themes of community building.

Community building is an overarching conceptual framework, not a program or technique.

Community building is variously described as a principle, framework, approach, or set of values that can and should underlie all community change work. Community building is not so much *what* is done to improve neighborhoods but rather *how* the work is done. It emphasizes community input and self-determination, attention to justice and equity, development of skills and knowledge, and connections among people and organizations.

Evidence that a community-building approach exists, therefore, comes from the qualitative aspects of activities. For example, a staff member who views his or her work through a community-building lens becomes more attentive to cultural differences among program participants and more appreciative of clients' strengths and assets. At the organizational level, governance structures encourage residents to serve as staff or board members. At the community level, the initiative's structure emphasizes broad-based local planning and collaboration among groups.

Community building is not an abstract concept; it contains concrete elements.

Based largely on the experiences of the last decade, practitioners and other change agents have defined community building as encompassing the following core activities:

❖ *Building the knowledge and abilities of individuals,* through leadership training, services and supports, skills development, and employment

❖ *Creating relationships* among residents through which they share emotional, psychological, and material support and can mobilize for collective action

❖ *Strengthening community institutions*—from formal public institutions and private enterprises to informal networks, associations, and religious, civic, or cultural groups—so they can respond to local concerns and promote general well-being

❖ *Creating links between institutions* so they can work collectively to improve the community

Recent community-change efforts have made these activities concrete in two ways. First, they have increased the quantity and quality of supports by funding new and better services, programs, and organizational development, often by appropriating good practices from other fields. Second, they have built individual and institutional abilities, created interpersonal relationships, and strengthened ties across stakeholder groups. For CCIs, these outcomes are the result of carrying out the initiative's core elements: developing a vision, articulating goals, creating a work plan, performing the work, and assessing achievements.

Resident engagement promotes trust and legitimacy.

From the outset, CCIs face a fundamental dilemma: The change process is meant to be of, by, and for the community, but initiatives typically are launched by people and institutions outside the community. The challenge for externally triggered initiatives is to create a process that is viewed as legitimate, trustworthy, and responsive to community concerns.

Bringing residents and community groups into an initiative and preparing them to lead the change process helps to make a CCI's efforts legitimate, both within and outside the neighborhood. As one resident noted, "Residents sell programs to other residents because of the trust factor. . . . Lack of engagement creates a bunch of underutilized programs."

> "The residents we work with have legitimacy in the community and know what their neighbors want and need. They know how something will 'sell' in the community and how to put it out there. They are our frontline and definitely add value to the final product."
>
> —CCI director

Resident involvement also gives CCIs access to information about the community's needs, strengths, and internal dynamics—what one observer called "real, lived experience." That information, which otherwise might not be available to outsiders, is invaluable for strategic planning and program development.

Resident engagement is crucial, but not all the time or in every aspect of the work.

Most stakeholders agree it is vitally important to have residents participate in program planning, design, governance, and oversight. In fact, resident membership on governing boards has been a hallmark of CCIs since their inception, and it is typically mandated in the initiative's design.

After more than a decade of experience, however, some practitioners conclude that not all aspects of community building require continuous investment by residents all of the time, especially the more operational and technical dimensions of the work. In the words of one funder,

> It's a technical process of taking people from the broad vision to the strategies for getting there, to the point of getting concrete about what the outcomes need to be. Who can do it? You need a savvy staff with very good consultants to do it. You can't train the staff and the community at the same time. You need the staff to do the technical plan, and they can do it without undermin-

ing the capacity-building process. Why make them [residents]
muddle through when we have the tools to move it faster? We
can do it in a respectful way.

It takes continuous effort and a deliberate focus to involve residents. It also takes a considerable investment of time and funding and a commitment to holding other stakeholders responsible for supporting residents in meaningful roles. Experience from many initiatives suggests that resident engagement often cycles up and down, with periods of high involvement followed by a lull in which activities are more staff-driven.

Community-building approaches have strengthened neighborhood leadership, connections among residents, and organizations' capacities and connections, but the link between those assets and improved community-level outcomes is not well documented.

Evaluations of CCIs and related initiatives demonstrate that new leaders have emerged, new relationships have formed among individuals, participating organizations have become stronger, and various kinds of community collaboration have occurred. Evaluations of CCIs do not yet demonstrate that these changes lead to broader community well-being across a range of indicators. Nonetheless, practitioners hold deep convictions that these community-building activities matter, and they support their view with case studies and anecdotal evidence. There is a limited body of research that suggests that there are correlations between desired community-building outcomes, such as social capital, and improved neighborhood conditions. However, most evaluations have not directly measured the effects of community building or its impact on social and economic progress in neighborhoods.

REVISITING COMPREHENSIVENESS AND COMMUNITY BUILDING

If comprehensiveness and community building are valid guiding principles, why haven't we accomplished more? In the words of one practitioner, "the spirit was willing but the body was weak." Because CCIs' agendas were so large, communities had to define them in manageable ways, and the broad principles inevitably became narrower in their execution.

In some cases, for instance, the comprehensiveness mandate came to mean developing a neighborhood plan with many programmatic elements. The challenges associated with integrating those programs on an ongoing basis, fostering synergistic results, and linking with factors beyond the neighborhood were so great that those dimensions of comprehensiveness receded into the distance. In other cases, the initiatives became preoccupied (or perhaps content) with engaging residents in the visioning process and developing the skills of those who became directly involved in the work. The broader community-building agenda was simply too much to address.

Part of the problem is that the core principles only acquire meaning when they are expressed in actions. Lacking a blueprint for how to change a neighborhood through a comprehensive community-building approach, CCI practitioners have had to develop strategies as they go. They know a great deal more now than they did a decade ago about how the principles play out in practice, and they are more experienced in staying true to them over time. Practitioners also know much more about the processes and supports that are required to put community-change efforts into place and make them work, including development of a community vision and plan for action, good governance and management, staffing, technical assistance, evaluation, and funding.

While practitioners, funders, residents, and other local stakeholders generally believe that the concepts of comprehensiveness and community building should continue to guide their efforts, they also realize that the next stage of theory and practice must resolve two crucial dimensions of community change: how to develop communities' capacity to do the work, and how to address the external structures that affect communities, including resources, systems, and barriers.

Both of those dimensions of community change were part of the original conception of CCIs, but most people assumed they would occur naturally in the course of community building around a comprehensive agenda. What, after all, is "community building" if not a way to think deliberately about strengthening the resources and abilities within a community? What is a "comprehensive" agenda if not a strategy for improving all of the factors that shape residents' experiences? In practice, however, CCIs fell short on both counts.

IN MANY WAYS, THE ANSWERS TO THESE QUESTIONS LIE IN THE capacities, connections, and actions of participants in each level of the ecology of change: individuals, neighborhood organizations and institutions, support providers, and entities engaged in policy issues, advocacy, and broad institutional reform. Chapters III through VI explore each of those dimensions respectively.

III.

Strengthening the Capacities and Connections of Community Residents

A MBITIOUS GOALS FOR COMMUNITY CHANGE MUST BE BACKED up by sufficient capacities and resources to make the goals achievable. The authors of a recent book define *community capacity* as:

> *the interaction of human capital, organizational resources, and social capital existing within a given community that can be leveraged to solve collective problems and improve or maintain the well-being of that community. It may operate through informal social processes and/or organized efforts by individuals, organizations and social networks . . . (Chaskin, Brown, Venkatesh & Vidal, 2001).*

The key features of communities with capacity, according to those authors, are a sense of community among residents, a commitment by residents to organize and act to improve the community, an ability to act to solve problems, and access to resources within and beyond the community.

The experiences of CCIs and other community-change efforts demonstrate a need for greater investment in developing the capacities of individuals, organizations, and support systems—the first three levels of participants in the ecology of change outlined in Chapter I—to promote broad community change. This chapter and the two that follow examine how that challenge plays out at each level. We do not examine every possible resource for change; rather, we focus on the kinds of strategies that are needed to pursue a comprehensive, community-building agenda. (Thus, for example, we do not discuss ideas for improving service programs for individuals but we do address issues surrounding how individuals might become leaders of community change.)

Because residents are the core of a community's assets, they represent the first level in the ecology of community change. As both agents and beneficiaries of community change, they can play a central role in shaping, implementing, and sustaining the change agenda. In many low-income communities, however, residents lack opportunities and support for those roles. Efforts by recent community-change ventures to increase residents' capacity involve *developing them as leaders, creating social connections, and organizing people to participate in change.* This chapter focuses on the promise and the challenge embedded in each of those activities. The overall message is that there is a vital need to invest much more deliberately, strategically, and generously in building individual residents' capacities in order for meaningful change to occur.

DEVELOPING LEADERS

Leadership development has always been a fundamental part of community building because it has such potential to improve individuals' circumstances and enhance their collective ability to undertake and sustain positive change. While it has always been a priority, leadership development has gained increasing prominence within the change process. One funder, reflecting on her years of grantmaking in the health field, recently commented:

> *A missed opportunity overall was our inadequate recognition of the need to invest in local leadership—not just physician leadership, but also in nursing, in public health, in lay leadership in*

distressed areas. We probably could have made more progress if we had given greater emphasis to building capacity on the community level (Hearn, 2001).

Our definition and discussion of leadership development draws heavily from a recent publication on community capacity (Chaskin, Brown, Venkatesh & Vidal, 2001), which describes the following characteristics:

[Leadership development] attempts to engage the participation and commitment of current and potential leaders, provide them with opportunities for building skills, connect them to new information and resources, enlarge their perspectives on their community and how it might change, and help them create new relationships.

There is no blueprint for developing local leaders. Methods range from formal training programs, which convey information or develop particular skills, to on-the-job training in which participants become members of boards or planning teams, serve in apprenticeships or co-staffing positions, and receive coaching or other training that prepares them to assume new roles. These approaches can be used to cultivate individual leaders or cadres of individuals who can participate in any stage of the community-change process: developing the overall vision, creating the plan for change, performing activities to implement the plan, tracking progress, and spreading the news about results.

Variation among communities produces different leadership needs and resources in different places, but the following observations are relevant to all community-change efforts.

It is essential to examine the community's existing leadership structures—both informal and formal—carefully. Their dynamics and subtleties are hard for outsiders to grasp easily.

Without deep knowledge of the local context, it can be difficult to identify and work with local leaders. Often, however, community-building initiatives select residents to participate on governance boards or in leadership training programs without knowing whether they are actually connected to appropriate constituencies or whether other neighborhood stakeholders will view them as legitimate.

Moreover, the relative strengths and weaknesses of old and new leaders present both assets and challenges. Existing leaders can bring credibility, experience, and extensive relationship networks to the table, but they also may suspect the motives and abilities of new leaders and jealously guard their "turf." New leaders contribute fresh ideas and energy and can increase the total number of leaders involved, but their skills may take time and resources to develop. Community-change efforts that do not recognize these dynamics risk creating conflict, failing to maximize the strengths of local leaders, and losing residents' willingness to make genuine investments in the initiative.

Participation in an initiative by local leaders does not always guarantee that neighborhood views receive respect.
Many of the technical skills required to improve housing, economic opportunities, and other program areas do not exist in communities depleted by long-term disinvestment. But when outside experts come in to help, residents sometimes feel that their own leadership skills have been discounted. As one resident said:

> *Leadership happens by being connected to the residents. You get a bond with the resident, you are out in the community, you talk with the people and you take questions, and they see your commitment and then they put you there [in a position of leadership]. They look up to you. But when you get to the table with these outside folks, you are nobody.*

The result, as one resident said, is that leaders are not operating on "an even playing field . . . professionals know how to work a meeting and talk in acronyms." Overwhelmed by professional service providers or community development practitioners, residents can fall silent and allow others to make the decisions.

Successful community building assumes that the outside expert's role is to share knowledge so that good decisions are made, but not to make the decisions. "What poor people experience every day in the world is people who won't respect their intelligence and who won't follow their lead," noted one observer. "The tragic cycle can be broken only if one recognizes the intelligence and capacity to lead of uneducated and sometimes damaged people."

Simply giving residents leadership roles, without training or follow-up, does not necessarily produce effective or powerful leaders.

According to several initiative directors, residents need extra support to help them stay at the table effectively: "They need the pre-meeting meeting that helps them develop their strategies, and then they need the post-meeting meetings to help them debrief and compare perspectives."

One way to develop local leaders is to give residents jobs as staff or board members. Often, however, the residents placed in those positions serve only as outreach workers or in roles for which they are not initially qualified. They may not receive the training or opportunities they need to develop competent leadership skills or to move up within the organization.

Formal training for local leaders—on how to run meetings or monitor agency spending, for example—is difficult to do well, however. Classes are an efficient way to share information and skills, but they can seem abstract, leaving residents feeling lost, and they often fail to provide adequate follow-up. Leadership development appears to be more successful when it comes as part of the process of addressing goals. As one technical assistance provider explained, "Rather than doing board training about board-staff relations, we did it around the hiring of an executive director, which was the task of the moment. Or we gave them financial training when we needed to build a budget."

The idea of "becoming leaders through the work" resonates with many residents; it is an approach that builds confidence and generates positive relationships among people who share a common goal. However, it is challenging to implement because it requires professional staff to consider everything on two levels: how to get the task done and how to exploit the task's teaching potential.

Some organizations have made serious commitments to developing resident leaders on the job, even if it means slowing down the pace of production, with an eye toward ultimately decreasing reliance on people from outside the community. One organization, for example, raised funds so that residents on staff could get the education they needed to take over leadership responsibilities from the non-resident professional staff; now, 60 of 75 staff are lifetime neighborhood residents.

Leadership development is an ongoing, intentional process.
The local leadership base rarely stays stable over time. Individuals
burn out, move into positions of higher authority, or leave the community, creating a constant pressure to replenish the leadership base.
It takes continuous investment and commitment to make sure that
new leaders develop and find roles to fill, even if existing leaders fail
to step aside.

CREATING SOCIAL CONNECTIONS

Relationships are crucial to the change process, both among neighborhood residents and between residents and individuals outside the
community. The work of strengthening these relationships is central
to the notion of community building; participants often describe it as
"reweaving the social fabric," "building social capital," "expanding
social networks," or "making connections."

Resident mobility, family disruption, changing neighborhood
demographics, and concerns about crime and safety have weakened
traditional social networks and communal supports in urban neighborhoods. Economic and political isolation exacerbates the social
isolation. And people who are isolated have fewer chances to learn
from others about resources and opportunities and how to access
them. They are less likely to see a way to exert control over the larger
forces affecting their lives, either alone or with others who share similar circumstances. Conversely, relationships among neighbors can
reduce isolation, help people cope with hardship and stress, and foster a sense of well-being. People who have social relationships "change
the way they see themselves and others. They can overcome a sense of
isolation and powerlessness," according to the board member of one
initiative.

Community-building strategies aim to develop and strengthen
the relationships that give residents social support, including com-
panionship, emotional sustenance, and information or practical help
such as child care and transportation. Techniques for strengthening
these connections include: community outreach; creation of tenants'
groups and block clubs; door-to-door organizing; resident involvement in group activities, services, planning processes, and decision-
making bodies; and mobilization of large groups of people for direct

action. Little systematic information exists about the effect of these activities on aggregate indicators of community well-being, but considerable anecdotal and experiential evidence points to the importance of social connections in the following ways.

Many local practitioners and residents believe that the process of creating social connections is an end in itself, especially in neighborhoods where residents are isolated and lack social support.

Relationships that provide mutual support go a long way toward alleviating the stress that residents of poor communities experience every day, and some practitioners say these social connections are as important as other outcomes for people whose lives have been devastated by the severe conditions of distressed communities. In the words of one community worker,

> People who have lost their sons—no amount of money would heal them. . . . These women don't need the solution that is given by experts. Many things can't be solved by a 501(c)(3) or a program. But at least I could figure out a way to bring them together so they could support each other.

For people living in intense emotional pain, simply having a friend to talk to can make a huge difference in the quality of life and their motivation to improve it. Yet initiatives often lose sight of the healing process in the rush to achieve tangible outcomes.

Social connections can establish a basis for civic activity by fostering a sense of community identity, spirit, and pride that crosses boundaries of age, race, and economic class.

People who aim to build community assume that civic participation will grow if individuals care about their neighbors and believe that their fellow-residents are disposed to care about them. Many community-change ventures sponsor social events such as block parties, neighborhood clean-ups, cultural evenings, or holiday celebrations to enhance residents' sense of belonging to and investment in the community.

Divisions among stakeholders, sometimes defined by racial and socioeconomic differences, make it hard for some to see how their own well-being could be linked with that of their neighbors.

Consequently, they may see little value in forging relationships. But as one representative of an intermediary organization said, "You have to have relationships for the sake of relationships because they keep people at the table."

For that reason, some leaders of community-change initiatives try to unify diverse constituencies through intensive group planning and visioning processes, such as group retreats, action teams, and ongoing dialogues. Although the relationships don't ensure success, they do provide vital building blocks. For example, researchers have found that urban neighborhoods with high levels of "collective efficacy"— mutual trust among neighbors, combined with willingness to intervene on behalf of the common good—have less violence than neighborhoods with low levels of this resource (Sampson, Raudenbush & Earls, 1997). Many community-change efforts have incorporated this lesson by using block clubs and neighborhood crime watches to build connections among residents.

Social connections can link distressed neighborhoods to resources and opportunities outside the community.

Many community-change efforts promote personal ties in order to help residents connect with job networks, for example, or share solutions for child care and transportation needs. Links between community members and city-wide advocacy groups can similarly help the neighborhood get its fair share of resources.

MOBILIZING PEOPLE TO PARTICIPATE IN COMMUNITY CHANGE

CCIs and other community-building endeavors emphasize outreach, resident engagement, and community mobilization. The underlying philosophy is that partnership, collective problem solving, and alliances with sources of power help to produce change. Some people criticize recent community-building efforts for their consensual approach to organizing, suggesting that it draws on a naïve analysis of power dynamics. We will revisit this issue in Chapter VI, when we discuss connections between communities and external sources of power. In the meantime, the experiences of recent efforts to mobilize communities offer the following observations at the resident level.

The goal of community mobilization should not be to engage all residents or to involve everyone in the same way. Those who want to participate will have different levels of interest and ability to commit.

Some residents want to be involved in their communities and will contribute deeply to community-building activities. Others don't have the time or interest, while still others may doubt their right to participate or their ability to do so. Some residents will not want to go to meetings on a regular basis but can be counted on in a crisis or for specific activities. Others will not want anything to happen without them, making them reliable but sometimes overbearing collaborators. Some want to be involved but have a single overriding interest, which may need to be managed. Some, described by a CDC director as "deep stakeholders," can be relied on throughout the course of the work. Further, over time a resident may play many roles depending on opportunity, interest, and need.

It is important to appreciate these differences and respond to them by finding more than one way for people to get involved in community building. One CCI developed its management and administrative structures on parallel tracks, for example, and found that "the impatient folks went to the action committee and the patient people to the governance committee."

Recent immigrants can be particularly hard to reach, especially the large population of undocumented residents. Successful strategies include reaching out through cultural groups, social clubs, and religious organizations. Much of the work with immigrants begins with rights-related work, letting immigrants know about what protections they have and what services they can tap into.

Community mobilization takes deliberate, sustained effort and has natural ebbs and flows.

Experienced community organizers know that participant involvement has crests and troughs. In the words of one organizer, the challenge is to figure out how to "take the bottom out of the cycle." One reason is that residents of poor communities tend to be very mobile. Some therefore have little commitment to their community; those who do become engaged are lost as local resources when they move on to a new neighborhood (although that community may benefit).

Still, notes one longtime CDC director, "When things settle down you have the old faithful."

Some vehicles for mobilization attract more and deeper participation than others. In general, neighborhood events, newsletters, and town meetings are not sufficient to get a broad base of residents involved on a continuing basis. CCIs have learned from experience that real community organizing takes door-to-door work: talking to individual residents, conducting household surveys, meeting in living rooms. Some leaders believe that the most successful resident engagement initiatives are the ones that *only* do community organizing—but even they require ongoing, intensive effort over the long term. "You can't just do it in the beginning and forget about it," a CDC director warned.

Some suggest that resident mobilization for community building follows an informal sequence. One funder described an example about school reform as follows:

> *People get involved because they're interested in their child. That's the hook. . . . they need support to understand how the school system works and connect them with other parents concerned with the same thing, to help them understand and listen to the other issues connected with their concern. They need basic knowledge on how things work, how the political system works and how to get involved with it in their community. Then they begin to see, hey, if I can make a difference for my child, then we can collectively make a difference on all kinds of issues in the community. They begin to understand levels of influence.*

Despite the knowledge that resident organizing is a key to community change, there are few reliable sources of funding for that activity. Many initiative leaders say their funders would rather support specific program areas.

RESIDENTS CAN BE POWERFUL ACTORS IN THE COMMUNITY-CHANGE process, but day-to-day implementation of a comprehensive community-building agenda also requires community groups and institutions that can turn residents' goals into reality. Those frontline organizations form our second level of participants in the ecology of community change, and their capacity for comprehensive community building is the focus of the next chapter.

IV.

STRENGTHENING THE CAPACITIES AND CONNECTIONS OF COMMUNITY INSTITUTIONS

NEIGHBORHOOD ORGANIZATIONS AND INSTITUTIONS FORM THE second level of participants in the ecology of community change. The experiences of recent CCIs and other community-change efforts suggest that these entities need considerable capacity building, both in their internal functions and in their ability to connect to other neighborhood stakeholders. As one participant put it, "We too often have ideas chasing capacity rather than the other way around."

The local organizations that participate in community change have very broad responsibilities, because they serve and represent residents in many ways. They are conduits through which residents can gain access to support systems, new resources, and opportunities to develop skills.

Local organizations that can promote a truly comprehensive community-change agenda are rare, however, especially in poor neighborhoods. As the leader of an intermediary organization put it:

How much capacity is really out there in the community? All organizations are undercapitalized, and even the strongest organizations in my community are without the capacity to do these new huge agendas. We need to look carefully at the health and structure of the organizations that are going to be doing this work in the community.

Investments to date have not solved the problem. The amount of money available falls short of the vast need for improvement among neighborhood institutions. Most funders would rather support programming than the development of unglamorous infrastructure. Many grants carry restrictions that limit the administrative fee organizations can charge on contracts and programs, which leaves the recipients barely able to manage their work—let alone build infrastructure.

Yet if community organizations are to be healthy, stable, and effective, they need good leadership, staffing, and coordination. And if they hope to achieve ambitious community-wide goals, they also need strong collaborative relationships and the ability to identify and address the racial and cultural dimensions of community change. The observations that follow explain how the people directly involved in community organizations view these essential ingredients for community change.

LEADERSHIP AROUND A COMMUNITY-WIDE AGENDA

Our first concern is with the leadership role played by the organization in the community (not, at this point, leadership within the neighborhood organization). Institutions that serve communities are driven both by their mission and their constituents. Being true to the goals of their mission gives organizations accountability; seeking input from an active and engaged constituency, and responding appropriately, gives them legitimacy. Much of a neighborhood organization's ability to lead a community-wide agenda, therefore, comes from its ability to represent the community's voice and its connections with key stakeholders within the community.

A community orientation does not necessarily come naturally for neighborhood organizations. It sometimes implies a new way of doing business.

Community-building goals require organizations to consider every action through the lens of how it helps to develop leadership, social

capital and networks, and collaboration. For example, participants
need to ask:

> *Does the organizational development effort somehow nurture,*
> *enhance, or multiply individual skills and talents? Does it pro-*
> *vide a forum for bringing people together to identify and act*
> *upon common goals? Does it contribute to an organizational*
> *infrastructure in the community that is collaborative, inclusive,*
> *and responsive to a range of key local needs (Chaskin, Brown,*
> *Venkatesh & Vidal, 2001)?*

Strong community-oriented organizations learn to move beyond
their own mission and fill a broader role. They not only lead the
development of a vision for community change, they also build
neighborhood residents' commitment to the vision, through outreach, targeted communication, and community organizing. Some go
further and explicitly define their mission as "community empowerment," meaning that they try to build residents' skills, leadership, and
relationships and work toward more equitable power relationships.
Such organizations engage residents in decision making at all levels,
at all times. "It's collective decision making, not just another layer of
representative government," explained the director of one community-
building organization.

**Good leadership involves very intentional efforts to coordinate
activities and connect projects. That coordination won't happen
without an organizational culture that insists on such connections and a management infrastructure that devotes time and
resources to developing them.**
Coordination must occur at the conceptual level as well as on the
ground. Managers need a framework for thinking about change that
helps them see the big picture and shows how all the pieces contribute
to an overarching strategy. They then need to communicate that
vision to the departments or individuals responsible for implementing specific projects. According to some staff directors, it is especially
important to designate an individual or part of the organization to
"think about maintaining an overall vision and think strategically
about connections."

Many organizations find it hard to maintain a consistent focus on
connecting with constituents, however, even those with deep roots

in the community. The barriers are a combination of funders' constraints, biases within the field or industry, and the absence of necessary skills among leaders and staff. In the case of CDCs, for instance, funding trends encouraged a narrow focus on producing low-income housing; consequently, the organizations were staffed primarily by people with technical expertise in crafting housing deals. This left CDCs less responsive to constituents' other needs, which in turn weakened their capacity to work on comprehensive community change. The challenge for leaders of these organizations is to reconnect with their communities and earn constituent credibility, buy-in, and participation. In the words of one longtime CDC director,

> *It's part of our mission, but we were losing touch with the community. We have been relatively successful over the years: we've built 750 units of housing in nine communities and we have 500 units in the pipeline. But we were still getting beat up. We were losing touch with community. We went through one-year of rethinking and decided to dedicate ourselves to community building, to working with the community on their agenda and not necessarily our agenda. We decided to use our talents and resources to create a bigger leadership base.*

Similarly, many social service agencies have limited institutional capacity when it comes to connecting with their communities. Critics blame their focus on individuals' deficits rather than on community-wide assets and empowerment. As a senior leader in the human services notes, "Social work organizations say the communities need more treatment services, whereas community builders are trying to get to a point where they'll have less need for the services." Leaders and staff of community organizations also find that service agencies seem to have a hard time relinquishing control to constituents or holding themselves as accountable to their clients as they are to their sources of money.

Changing an organization's orientation requires significant leadership and dedication. In the words of one director of a community organization, "How do you go back and recreate yourself if you've been in existence for 20–25 years?" It can mean a completely new way of operating.

Being responsive means adopting a different view of institutional accountability.

The good intentions expressed in an organization's mission will not, by themselves, ensure responsiveness to the community. In the words of an experienced evaluator, "[responsiveness] requires a 'genetic predisposition' but is triggered by the presence of environmental factors." Those factors might come from the outside, in the form of incentives from funders or catastrophic events that become catalysts for action, or they might come from within.

If organizations pursue whatever money is available, they can wind up developing projects that aren't aligned with their core mission. Because project funding usually carries restrictions on how the money can be used, it may be hard to instill community-building priorities into these programs or connect them with other activities. Instead, according to people on the frontlines of this work, organizations need to evaluate every opportunity against their core mission. They should be clear enough about what they are doing, and why, that they are willing to forgo money offered for projects that don't advance community-building goals.

> "Changing behavior is hard. . . . It's about being accountable in a different way and about whose interests an organization is representing. Where I've seen movement, the changes happened not because of external funding but because the staff were committed to it."
>
> —Evaluator

Although some of the work of CCIs and other community-building endeavors has focused specifically on helping community organizations make this transition, few have fully adopted a different way of doing things or a different way of relating to stakeholders.

STAFFING OF NEIGHBORHOOD ORGANIZATIONS

Staff directors, residents, technical assistance providers, and other intermediaries interviewed for this book all said that developing skilled, knowledgeable staff (including those who lead neighborhood groups) is crucial to overcoming the "fragility" of community-based organizations. Hiring, training, and retaining good staff are therefore constant issues for community-development and community-building initiatives. "In the end, it's all about staffing," said the director of an intermediary:

> *The success or failure of your work depends on who's doing it. And I've come to the conclusion that what you need are staff who know how to do deals.... You need staff who know who's got to be at the table and can get them there, staff who know where the money is and how to leverage it. That's what separates the men from the boys in this field... and the women from the girls!*

Good staff have an array of skills, knowledge, and personal qualities that are hard to find. Sometimes, those attributes are strongest in neighborhood residents.

The first challenge is to find staff, and enough of them, with the right skills for the work at hand. Directors of organizations or initiatives must be adept at translating vision into action; moving projects forward; connecting discrete projects under an overarching goal; monitoring progress; and maintaining good relations with funders, stakeholders, residents, and collaborators. Frontline staff must possess the technical skills, community knowledge, and passion needed for community building work—a broad order that is hard to fill.

It is notable that many practitioners and residents say they value staff's "passion," "heart," "caring," and "concern" over technical expertise or professional degrees. For that reason, many believe strongly that community members are the best candidates to become agents of neighborhood change. They advocate creating paid opportunities for residents to contribute their experience, knowledge, and social connections to the work of community organizations. Some executive directors of community organizations agree that residents make exceptional staff members, and they use mentoring, job shadowing, and job partnering to train residents for that role. Explained one director, "We find it easier to get technical training for a person who knows and understands our community and our organization than to take a professionally trained person and turn them into a community builder."

Other practitioners are skeptical about the value of having untrained residents fill positions that require technical knowledge. They suggest that the most appropriate place for residents who lack specific expertise is on the governing board, where they can address issues of overall vision and direction.

Chronically low salaries are a common barrier to finding and retaining high-quality staff.

Community-based organizations often face pressure from private funders, government backers, and even their constituents to limit salaries so that more of their budget can support programs. Many provide only minimal benefits such as health care, flexible hours, and vacations. The low pay makes it hard to recruit qualified staff and, according to some practitioners, demeans the profession and practice of community building. Uncompetitive salaries for institutional staff also seed resentment about the higher salaries paid to technical assistance providers, staff of intermediary organizations, evaluators, and funders.

Some organizations have found creative ways to augment professional staff with low-paid or volunteer labor, such as VISTA volunteers, recent college graduates, interns, retirees, and neighborhood residents. These techniques diminish staffing problems but do not resolve them.

Low salaries contribute to another issue that undermines neighborhood organization's capacity: staff retention. Burnout is a constant threat; community workers put in long hours, and much of their work occurs after normal business hours and on weekends. Turnover also is high because there are few internal career ladders or opportunities for promotion and advancement. It is not uncommon for staff members who want to advance to move on to another organization.

Staff must be trained not only in administrative duties but also to recognize community assets and capacities and to incorporate them into the work of community building.

Staff skills need constant development and upgrading, especially in the areas of administration, finance, human resource management, board interactions, and strategic planning. Practitioners advocate training programs that teach both technical information and the skills involved in community building and organizing. A growing number of community colleges, other undergraduate programs, and graduate schools offer training in community building or community development. Most of these attempt to synthesize curricula from the social sciences, management sciences, and schools of professional practice. Some training programs develop in partnership with community groups; others bring residents into the classroom to serve as instructors.

Because people bring their personal biases about poor neighborhoods to the work of community building, staff training should help workers understand and appreciate local assets. For example, a senior staff member of a settlement house noted that her organization puts staff through exercises that examine their attitudes:

> *We explore what settlement house participants are capable of and what needs to be in the staff's domain. We draw on the idea that the staff are part of the community and that some are also former participants in programs. . . . Our position is that everyone has something to give. It's a whole different way of starting to operate from a traditional social service agency.*

COLLABORATION

Collaboration enables organizations to pursue agendas beyond the reach of any one institution. It also connects them with a broad group of stakeholders who have similar goals and constituents in the community.

Collaborations can take several forms. They can be informal or formal agreements, narrowly focused on a specific goal or dedicated to broad issues, voluntary or mandated, ongoing or episodic. They may involve formal case management or arrangements that "broker" services from various agencies. All of these relationships translate into efforts to help participants in one program get support from other programs operated by the initiative or by a collaborating agency.

Project directors report some success in getting organizations or departments that had no history of collaboration to plan projects jointly and agree on some common target outcomes and approaches. There is no evidence yet, however, that those efforts will result in better outcomes for individual residents or entire neighborhoods.

Some early CCIs were accused of having a "romantic" notion of collaboration. Their leaders appreciated how collaboration could address a range of issues, and they valued its consensual orientation, but they were naïve about the complexities of local power dynamics and they underestimated the costs of a collaborative approach. That experience suggests the following themes.

Collaboration can be costly in terms of political capital and the scarce resources of time and energy. Community organizations should therefore reserve collaboration for times when it is clearly the best strategy to pursue.

A collaborative arrangement inevitably changes the power dynamics within a neighborhood. Residents can gain a stronger voice, and public institutions can find new ways of sharing work, authority, and responsibility. But each collaborator also gives up some degree of control over decisions which, in turn, can exacerbate existing tensions or create new jealousies among local groups. Competition for scarce resources, turf issues, fears about being taken over by other organizations, and differences in priorities all make it difficult to rearrange the distribution of power.

To overcome these barriers, people have to believe that collaboration is in their self-interest, and they have to trust their fellow collaborators. But in neighborhoods where initiatives come and go, disrupting local relationships and power structures, people often are protective of their own organizations and distrustful of others. There may be intense competition for resources and roles, and dynamics of race, culture, and economic class may complicate efforts to collaborate.

In such an environment, people need help staying at the table long enough to change the power dynamic. There are no clear lessons about the best ways to support this process, but the characteristics of some successful collaborations offer a few hints:

❖ Collaborators feel like equals despite differences in their resources and assets.

❖ Collaborators clearly articulate their own interests in the partnership and negotiate roles and responsibilities with each other at the outset.

❖ Collaborators work toward a common view and a fair division of labor, which maximizes each partner's strengths and minimizes the differences.

❖ Collaborators share ownership of the effort and have a long-term, mutual investment in its outcomes.

❖ Commitment to the partnership endures despite turnover within organizations or local government.

❖ The accountability process is clearly defined, including expectations for each organization.

❖ A structure exists for shared decision making and governance that gives community members some authority.

❖ The collaboration is not established to circumvent or compete with existing governance entities.

Because collaboration is such a complex and costly undertaking, it is not the answer to every problem. It may be possible to move forward on certain agenda items without a fully democratic institutional collaboration. Moreover, the cost-benefit tradeoff is likely to be different for different types of institutions. Weak, financially strapped organizations, for example, may have a great deal to gain from collaboration with stronger partners, but the relative cost to them in terms of staff time, political capital, and internal capacity also is likely to be greater.

EFFECTIVE GOVERNANCE
Neighborhood-based governance can be defined as "mechanisms and processes to guide planning, decision making, and implementation, as well as to identify and organize accountability and responsibility for action undertaken" (Chaskin & Garg, 1997). Effective governance is thus a cornerstone of the capacity needed to produce community change. But what does "effective governance" look like for community-change efforts?

No one form of governance works best in all circumstances. Sometimes a governance structure emerges naturally from the work, as leaders assume roles and responsibilities and form a group that sets rules for how to operate. The group's effectiveness depends on its legitimacy in the eyes of the community, its accountability to the community, and its ability to make decisions and get things done. Often, governance arrangements are more complex, especially when the work involves collaboration among several institutions or when the work is supported by an external funder.

People on the frontlines of community change make the following observations about effective governance.

Questions about who is responsible for decision making should be addressed at the beginning of a community-building effort.

There are many practical reasons to avoid governance decisions at the outset of a community-change initiative. People tend to avoid controversial issues when they are trying to build commitment around a shared agenda. The funder or lead agency may want to maintain sole control, or partners may believe that governance will emerge over time. The result is that institutions sometimes begin work without clear rules for decision making or accountability.

Practitioners have found that the lack of a widely accepted governing body (or at least a process for developing one) allows mistrust and resentment to fester in the community, and it diverts energy from the work of the change effort. This doesn't mean that a well-functioning governance entity must precede the work, just that people must agree on who has initial authority for each major area and how those roles may be renegotiated as the work matures.

Funders often are not well-positioned to dictate the form and/or membership of a governance body.

Without a deep understanding of neighborhood politics and history, or working relationships with community members, a funder is unlikely to appreciate the consequences of anointing specific leaders and giving them particular responsibilities. An uninformed appointment can polarize a community, or it might feed an ongoing power struggle.

It takes significant time and support to create a new governance body for community change, and the form governance takes may change as the work evolves.

Community-change efforts aim to be inclusive and collaborative, involving people and organizations both within and outside the community. All of these entities must have a voice in decisions and policies. However, few initiatives invest sufficiently in turning the disparate group of collaborators into an effective decision-making body. In fact, it is hard to identify cases in which diverse governance bodies have worked well over time. Sometimes one group—often the outside "movers and shakers"—disengages and simply stops coming to meetings; sometimes everyone stays engaged but residents do not sit at the table as equals.

Moreover, some processes are time-limited. The trick is to identify needs as they occur and select the best governance vehicle to meet that need. That doesn't always happen, however. For example, one initiative established resident teams to define its vision and priorities during the planning process, but when implementation began, the teams dispersed, and the initiative had no other way to include residents in decision making. By the time the community eventually became an Empowerment Zone (EZ), most residents were disengaged and cynical. Those who did gain some control in the EZ structure did not want to share it. Recalled one participant, "It was like trying to take a lollipop from a child who has been waiting for it for weeks."

One solution is to vest governance authority in more than one entity—to promote a "fluid and evolutionary" process, as a funder suggested. For example, different individuals or organizations may have more jurisdiction over planning, convening, and connecting the change effort to resources outside the community than for providing services. In this sense, as an experienced community builder observes, "Governance may be more about negotiating roles, responsibilities, and outcomes"—that is, the capacity for change—"as opposed to formal structures."

The use of more than one governance vehicle increases opportunities for participation. A single board, even a large one, cannot represent the community in all its diversity, and it has little incentive to reach out beyond the usual orbit and push for wider engagement.

"Vision keepers" can maintain the momentum of a community-wide agenda, but they have to supported by money and staff.
Many community-wide efforts are held together by a solitary person or organization with a daunting assortment of responsibilities. If that linchpin is removed, the capacity to keep all of the pieces on track disappears. Even if the leader remains, few individuals possess all of the skills needed to manage community change well. Thus an abiding challenge for CCIs and related initiatives is to reduce reliance on one key leader and develop capacity for producing and managing work within organizations or coalitions in the community. CCIs have done this, with varying degrees of success, through coaches, small work-groups, or advisory councils; through individuals or groups who keep the community vision focused over time; and via intermediary organizations that help to manage activities.

These vision keepers try to ensure that everything collaborators do is consistent with the initiative's goals and that the flurry of separate projects does not distract people from the big picture. Vision keepers play roles in these tasks:

❖ Developing an initial community plan

❖ Coordinating the work of partners and multiple projects

❖ Building and maintaining connections across projects and across organizations

❖ Raising funds and maintaining fiscal accountability

❖ Monitoring the progress of the participants in the overall endeavor

❖ Keeping an eye on the big picture

Establishing an intermediary structure to manage a community initiative has high payoffs, but it requires independent financing.
Many CCIs have used intermediary organizations to provide infrastructure for collaboration and to improve local organizations' capacity

to lead and participate in community change. Intermediaries play roles in linking funders, practitioners, and other stakeholders; managing initiatives; and educating both foundations and their grantees. The intermediary role can be integrated into the work of a lead agency, added to an organization's goals, or embodied by an independent institution that is created specifically to manage community-wide work.

Intermediaries can produce good results. Communities and initiatives that have established independent entities have reaped the benefits of improved accountability and central management. The approach is also risky, however. It takes money to establish a local intermediary. Because they cannot draw on program dollars to support their operations, intermediaries must be financed through foundation grants, membership dues, or fees for service. Further, the intermediary role requires staff to play many roles for many masters, and sometimes those roles produce conflicts of interest.

ATTENTION TO RACIAL AND CULTURAL ISSUES

Community building's core values include the promotion of racial justice and healthy intergroup relations. Attention to racial and cultural issues is also a prerequisite to successful work in distressed neighborhoods.

People affiliated with community organizations have experimented with anti-racism staff-training programs, curricula that emphasize the cultural competencies needed to do community work, language translation services for meetings, community cultural festivals, cross-cultural economic development strategies, and other methods for addressing the racial issues that surface among neighborhood groups and between institutions and residents. There is a growing sense, however, that the work around racism does not go deep enough and that the capacity to identify and address institutional and structural dimensions of racism is not infused throughout the work of community-building institutions. Practitioners note three persistent themes in particular.

Every participant in the change process needs to develop the capacity to talk about the deep and difficult aspects of racial issues.

Whites need to understand more clearly what white privilege is and how it affects disadvantaged communities. People of color need to address the tough issues that undermine their ability to act, including internalized racism and isolation. And all groups need to develop skill in tackling issues collectively, in racially mixed groups.

The capacity to confront racial issues head-on is important, because racial tensions can weaken the credibility and trust that are vital to the community-building process. The people consulted for this report illustrated that point in many ways. One practitioner described how the older, established leaders of his community refused to acknowledge his organization because they thought he "talked to too many white people." Only after the organization achieved results that residents cared about was he able to forge a relationship with them. A funder who is white found that resident trust did not "just happen" as a result

> "We need to look at how the fields have grown, the different roles that are called for, and figure out how to diversify throughout the field. Who's at the table? Who's not at the table? A small group makes the rules. How do you get other points of view there to shape and influence the field."
>
> —Foundation representative

of his good work and follow-through. The community's deep distrust came from years of being let down by institutions and a lack of faith in "the system." That funder learned that trust does not automatically stem from a few kept promises.

Neighborhood institutions have limited capacity to address institutional and structural racism or the ways that political, economic, and social privilege operate to marginalize people of color.

Despite the fact that so much community-building work occurs in communities of color, the people involved in community building often don't have the capacity to address issues of structural racism. As a result, some suggest, community-building work tends to proceed by addressing the symptoms of neighborhood distress, not by tackling the root causes of white privilege and structural racism. In the words of one practitioner, "We must teach people to be clear. There are differences between root causes and symptoms, and we must do this work around race and skin color."

People widely acknowledge the need to analyze and remove racial barriers to progress. But, observed one practitioner, funders are unlikely to support the goal of "getting rid of white supremacy"—and there are few forums where people can examine these underlying issues in thoughtful and constructive ways. (We explore this subject more thoroughly in Chapter VI.)

Racial inequities exist within and among local community-building organizations.

Across the board, practitioners agree that few community-based and intermediary organizations working in the field of community building are led by people of color. Those that are tend to be smaller and weaker than their white-led counterparts. The way in which funding works has reinforced this inequity. It is difficult for any organization to garner money for institutional development and ongoing general support, but organizations with no preexisting ties to foundations, no staff dedicated to fundraising, and no flexibility in their budgets face an extra disadvantage. Groups led by people of color rarely have the opportunity to catch up to their older, larger, and more-developed institutional partners (or competitors).

Residents, practitioners, and funders all appreciate the value of strong community-building organizations led and staffed by people of color, but they also recognize that those organizations require deliberate and generous investment in efforts to build leadership, knowledge, and skills.

COLLECTIVELY, THE INDIVIDUAL AND ORGANIZATIONAL CAPACITIES outlined in this chapter and the previous one lay a solid foundation for community building. But community change also is influenced by a third level of participants: the funders, technical assistance providers, researchers, and other outside organizations that support people and groups acting inside the neighborhood. The process of linking communities to that broader context is the subject of Chapter V.

V.

Strengthening the System of Supports

T HE THIRD LEVEL IN THE ECOLOGY OF COMMUNITY CHANGE encompasses organizations that provide resources and supports to community-change endeavors. These include funders, technical assistance providers, evaluators, and other producers of knowledge. Usually, these organizations are located outside the neighborhood. They work independently but in partnership with neighborhood institutions.

Some of these entities have adapted their work over the last decade to align better with both the content and values of comprehensive community building. But experience from recent CCIs and related community-change efforts suggests that the agenda for change at this level is incomplete. Moreover, the support providers who work hand in hand with community-building entities represent only a small, self-selected group. As such, they are not representative of all actors at this level in the ecology of change, but they have the potential to lead the way for their peers.

This chapter presents observations about four basic issue areas for support providers and the recipients of their services: *funding levels, purposes, and relationships; access to technical assistance; evaluation and strategic data use; and opportunities for knowledge development.*

FUNDING LEVELS, PURPOSES, AND RELATIONSHIPS

Community-building organizations need enough money to compensate staff and support programs. They need a reasonable reserve of funds so they can weather crises and withstand the vagaries of funders' cash flows. And they need flexible spending arrangements that allow them to act entrepreneurially—by seeding new projects, for example, or by taking advantage of a potential new stream of public funding. Unfortunately, a lack of connections to sufficient money has left community organizations financially starved, even while they are charged with solving enormous problems.

Foundations play vital leadership roles in funding comprehensive community change.

Foundations are virtually the only source of flexible funding for organizational development and broader community-building activities. The vital role of philanthropic money in community change implies that foundations have a responsibility to be innovative and risk-taking in their grants, and many participants criticize foundations for not stepping up to the plate. According to one former foundation official and longtime leader of community change,

> *I think all of us understand the importance of getting resources into the communities if capacity is to be built. When the market ran up in the '90s, foundations had the opportunity to do funding in a different way and to really have an effect on the field. They simply did not take advantage of it and they missed the opportunity. Instead, they just made more grants for initiatives. When they did make endowment grants, they were small.*

Even when foundations do take the lead in underwriting community change, it is often through "initiatives" such as CCIs rather than as part of regular and ongoing support for community-based organizations.

The biggest gap in funding is for core operations, the functions that are vital to community institutions' capacity. Few funders understand that core support is as important as money for programs and activities and that there is a continuous need to support capacity development.

Core operating support is not tied to a specific outcome. Rather, it supports an organization's basic existence, enabling people to improve and expand internal processes, coordinate activities, collaborate with other groups, and conduct strategic planning. Organizations that aim to change communities without core support have little leeway to experiment with new approaches and roles. As one director said, "There is not enough freedom in an organization to get people in a creative thinking mode."

Some analysts suggest that funding gaps have produced a field that is intrinsically weak. They note that the organizations on the frontlines of community building are plagued by a chronic lack of capacity, in all of the forms described in this book. Some funders have responded by offering more support for organizational development and for various kinds of short-term technical assistance. As many executive directors note, however, such funders are rare, and the amount of money they provide is insufficient. It takes substantial, ongoing support to make institutions truly capable of changing communities.

> **"Organizations are so dreadfully undercapitalized. Despite the geniuses that run them and all the [technical assistance] in the world, they can't do what they need to do until we change the funding streams to provide for greater organizational capacity."**
>
> **—Director of a community organization**

More funds must be specifically earmarked for community building.

The public and private sectors typically direct their money to social, economic, or physical development programs—isolated categories of work with short-term funding cycles—rather than comprehensive efforts to improve community life. Their support comes with tightly specified activities and outcomes that allow little room for the relationship development and outreach that constitute so much of community building. Activities that are especially hard to cover financially include community organizing, development of local leaders, advocacy for policy change, and other types of networking among individuals, groups, and sectors.

There has been some progress. Major philanthropies have entered the arena, even as others have left. Recent federal initiatives, such as the Empowerment Zone/Enterprise Community and HOPE VI initiatives, have made some public funding available for community-building activities. A scattering of states and cities have also committed funds for community improvement. Still, the goals and approaches of comprehensive community change have not infused the mainstream funding sources that feed community institutions. As a former funder noted,

> There came a point in the late 1980s when some foundation funding took on a new cast, moving beyond project funding to initiative funding directed toward the transformation of communities. . . . And now we've moved to a place where there is more government involved, locally and federally, and where there are more organic and varied initiatives. The question before us is how to support that variety.

Although CCIs usually receive money for longer periods than standard programs, the grant cycle is still too short.

Almost everyone interviewed for this book recognized a fundamental mismatch between the amount of time that real community change takes (at least 10–20 years) and funders' willingness to commit to long-term support. Although there are exceptions, most public and private funding expires after three to five years. As one former public official said, "The limited timeframe fits funders' needs rather than the needs of community change."

A long-term commitment is important because it frees directors and senior staff from time-consuming fundraising efforts. According to directors of community organizations, long-term funding also provides a sense of security that enables people to be more ambitious and experimental, qualities that help advance community-change efforts. And long-term funding creates a dynamic between funder and grantee that is closer to a partnership, with ups and downs that both sides work through over time. Explained one funder,

We were committed to investing in a neighborhood long-term. It was a terrible failure three years ago but now it is a success. We funded a weak lead agency that failed. Some of the funders in our group were ready to give up. But the commitment was to the neighborhood and so we stuck with it. Taking a long-term approach really changes things.

On the other hand, some people believe that predictable flows of money create dependency, reduce the incentive to produce high-quality and timely work, and gets organizations "hooked on a flow of money which is otherwise hard to get." Some funders believe it is healthier to create competition for funds among grantees.

By channeling much of their money for community building into "initiatives," funders create other problems.

Much of the recent support for community capacity has come in the form of initiatives—often CCIs but also efforts to improve specific program areas, such as employment, health, or education. As the first cycle of these initiatives draws to a close, the value of that strategy deserves scrutiny. On one hand, investors realize that fundamental capacity building is a necessary step toward achieving programmatic outcomes. On the other hand, they are reluctant to commit to long-term obligations to support community capacity building. Noted one practitioner,

Foundations know that capacity building has to accompany initiative funding. They assume that when the initiative goes away we won't need capacity-building funding any more. But we need it on an ongoing basis.

In many ways, the initiative structure solves this dilemma: investments in community capacity occur in a time-limited way around identifiable, funder-specified goals. Moreover, the benefits from the investment are likely to spill over into other aspects of the organization or community work. But neighborhood organizations come to rely on the new streams of money that initiatives provide, and they inevitably grapple with sustainability.

Funders have tried to react responsibly by developing exit strategies that anticipate the end of their initiatives. Grantees, too, have tried to think creatively about new types of unrestricted support—

through entrepreneurial activity or direct mail fundraising, for example. But the problem remains a significant one.

The power imbalances between funders and grantees are flashpoints for conflict.

Funders and grantees both recognize the difference in power between them. Regardless of how accessible, encouraging, and tactful a funder may be, the relationship between giver and receiver is intrinsically unequal. One has something that the other needs. One can decide what to do; the other's fate depends on that decision.

Many funders have tried to do business differently when it comes to community-building enterprises. But experienced practitioners say that grantees often find the "partnership" and "collaboration" language adopted by some funders to be disingenuous. As one director said,

> *Power relationships are unequal, so let's not pretend this is a partnership. Many other kinds of relationships are possible. But let's not have the fiction that all participants are equal. Funders like to say this is a more collaborative new approach, but they are still the people who sign the check. Grantee organizations still feel pushed around but don't want to say so. . . . It's very easy to say it's a new relationship, but it's just not so.*

Grantees also are skeptical of funders' statements that money is their least important contribution. As one director put it, "They are the only industry I know that claims that the core business they do is not the core business they do." Grantees sometimes feel that foundations are "gaming" them, and they would be more comfortable if the processes for decision making were more straightforward. "The dysfunctional piece happens when foundations are not up front about their expectations," one practitioner bluntly said. "It's better for the funder to be clear than to hint at something they want accomplished."

Many funders are aware of these problems. One agreed that it's important to be clear about intentions and expectations: "Sharing information helps to demystify the relationship and . . . equalize things. You need to make your decisions rules clear. It doesn't erase the power issues, but it makes them more manageable." Added another, "The power relationships never go away. We tried the partnership rhetoric but it didn't seem to translate well. . . . We have learned the need for everyone being clear about our expectations."

ACCESS TO TECHNICAL ASSISTANCE

The emphasis on comprehensiveness and community building in current initiatives has provoked a rethinking of the kinds of technical assistance needed to support community change. In general, organizations need access to technical support providers that are: knowledgeable about the organization, the neighborhood, and local and national contexts; technically proficient in their specialties and steeped in general principles of community building; respectful of the community's interests and circumstances; racially sensitive and culturally competent; objective and open-minded; able to tolerate ambiguity; and able to facilitate organizational change. Practitioners say that staff and board members of community organizations need ongoing technical support in the following four areas.

> **"It's important that the vibes be right. Not just the technical knowledge; respect and racial sensitivities are important."**
>
> **—CBO Director**

❖ *Technical skills and knowledge* related to designing, managing, and implementing projects. At an organization that develops community employment centers, for example, staff may need help identifying existing resources, conducting needs assessments, preparing clients for the workplace, and establishing relationships with employers.

❖ *Organizational development.* In most cases, community organizations need to strengthen their existing work as well as assume new roles. They often need help managing their growth, developing new administrative systems, governing the complex process of change, evaluating progress, communicating with stakeholders, and resolving conflicts.

❖ *Information about public and private service systems.* Individuals and organizations need to know how the systems that support and influence them work, how to take advantage of what they offer, and how to change them in positive ways.

❖ *The "process skills" of community building*, such as outreach, organizing, envisioning change, planning, and relationship building.

The community-building field has not yet solved the problem of how to provide appropriate, high-quality technical assistance. The operational factors that come into play—assistance providers' skills and sensitivity, the issues involved in timing support effectively, and systems for delivering technical assistance—are not within the scope of this book. But a few observations about supporting institutional capacity and connections bear discussion here.

Technical assistance must build organizations' internal capacity to lead and produce change, not just help with specific problems. Assistance providers need to impart skills and knowledge and also make the information relevant by applying it to the nuances of the work at hand. Peer-to-peer support seems especially valuable in this regard. For example, directors of community organizations report successes from asking local CDC directors to offer advice and guidance. These peers are "grounded, trustworthy, and familiar with what you do," said one director; "it allows for economies of scale." Arrangements that send people from one organization to another, especially residents, also help to build bonds and foster the cross-fertilization of ideas.

Coaching is another popular technique for supporting community organizations. Coaching relationships use assistance providers who are extremely familiar with an organization and its context to advise the executive director, board, or staff. Coaches offer a sounding board, a guiding hand, and a support system for leaders who feel isolated. Ultimately, however, their value lies in their ability to help participants find their own solution rather than in providing the solution themselves. In the words of one director, "A most valuable resource that we now have and rely on is the coaching; I don't know what we're going to do without it."

Recipients of technical assistance need to define their own capacity needs and manage their assistance providers.

Technical assistance is a boon to community institutions, but it can also be a burden. Rarely does a provider walk in the door and provide exactly the support an organization is looking for. More frequently, the organization's director must spend time and energy orienting the provider to the neighborhood, its issues, and the community-change initiative. As a director of a community organization observed,

> "There's a culture about technical assistance that's been developed. Here I am trying to deal with fires, and they want to have a nice leisurely conversation."
>
> **—Resident board member**

> You expect a technical assistance provider to help you, but they actually make more work for you. When I hire staff, I know I have to develop them. With technical assistance providers, I can't wait for them to come help me, but then it turns out that I have to develop an individual education plan for them. The person becomes a management issue.

Technical assistance that does not meet the criteria described above not only fails in its goal of supporting an organization, it can seriously undermine the organization's connections with the community. Some leaders tell painful stories of having to rebuild credibility within their neighborhoods after bringing the wrong assistance providers in to help with community building. "We got the technical assistance, but it really set us back," recalled one board member. "The whole process that we were trying to build in the community got unbuilt."

EVALUATION AND STRATEGIC DATA USE

Evaluation is a thorny process for social interventions, and CCIs have had their share of evaluation-related dilemmas, especially regarding the purposes and audiences of evaluation, the outcomes to be evaluated, the methods of evaluation, and the roles of evaluators. In complex initiatives, evaluation often is a lightning rod for tensions and unresolved issues around what outcomes are sought, what actions are taken, who is in charge, and how money is spent.

Ten years ago, CCI stakeholders were unsure of how to apply existing evaluation tools to the task of documenting and understanding the types of change to which CCIs aspired. In previous generations of social experiments, evaluations almost exclusively tracked programmatic outcomes and served as a tool of accountability between grantees and funders. Many of the community-building endeavors shifted the emphasis of evaluation to the other end of the spectrum, and implementation studies and process documentation began to dominate the evaluation literature.

CCIs have made important progress on the evaluation front, however, as evaluators clarified the challenges and the capacities associated with evaluations of complex, community-change efforts. Although much work remains to be done, CCI evaluations have made considerable headway on which outcomes to track, for what purposes, and for which audiences. The following observations stem from those experiences.

Long-term outcomes—statistically significant changes in community-wide indicators of child, family, and neighborhood well-being, in multiple domains—are unlikely to show up within most funders' timeframes. Identifying interim outcomes along the path to longer-term change, therefore, is a critical step.
By identifying the pathways they will use to achieve change, initiative planners can name the early results that will demonstrate whether an initiative is on track. Sometimes these are directly linked to long-term programmatic outcomes—for example, school readiness or job training. At other times, they are indirectly linked to long-term outcomes—for example, changes in community leadership, social capital, sense of local identity, and hope. Insofar as the pathways identify these elements as valid milestones, then the elements become markers of progress to be captured by evaluation.

A variety of stakeholders now realize that initiatives must be able to articulate pathways of change and base evaluations on them, but the task is difficult. For one thing, the process of community change is exceedingly difficult to map and track. Inadequate theory, a dearth of empirical evidence, and limited experience undermine the pathway mapping process. Moreover, defining the route that a comprehensive initiative will follow has political dimensions that are affected by neighborhood history, capacity, personalities, power arrangements, and negotiating skills. Even if the research base and tools were richer, more work would be needed to develop low-cost and accessible measures of many of the early and intermediate outcomes on the CCI agenda, especially around concepts of social capital and community capacity.

The emphasis on pathways does not suggest that the accountability dimension of evaluation should be dropped; stakeholders still need evidence that their investments are paying off. The important shift is in the link between activities and outcomes. As one funder explained,

> *We get some sense from our board that they want to see the impact of our grant making. But we provide general operating support, and it's hard to show impact because you can't see how your money works. There's got to be a balance between what you can see and the intangibles. It's easy to fund nonprofits to do a "thing." But you don't get any impression about the significance of the "thing." So you need to demonstrate the importance of both the tangibles and the intangibles.*

The focus on pathways of change has tilted the nature of evaluation away from a purely summative accounting of the initiative to a continuous process of feeding back information that can guide management and decision making.

The future for evaluation of community-building initiatives may be less about traditional evaluation and more about "knowledge management and development." It is a challenge for any organization to stay true to its core philosophy while also being nimble, flexible, and entrepreneurial—but it is easier when organizations are committed to reflecting on and learning from their experiences. Not every community-based organization needs to make this dimension a priority, but learning from feedback is an essential capacity for organizations involved in community building.

The term "learning organization" captures the institutional capacity that many stakeholders believe is so important. Being a learning organization means collecting, analyzing, and using information to plan activities, evaluate the organization's performance, understand the community's assets and needs, and share emerging lessons. "We have to acknowledge that this is a learning enterprise, and we need to establish systems to capture the learning," urged a longtime practitioner.

> "Evaluation results used to be secret until they were published. This created fear in staff. Now we [try] to convert evaluations and funding decisions into results as we go along. . . . This way, we can incorporate the learning into our business and make improvements before we are told to do so by funders."
>
> —CBO Director

CCIs have been conceived as opportunities to gather rich information about effective community revitalization strategies, and some evaluations have made the most of that potential for learning. Several CCI funders have invested significantly in evaluation and encouraged evaluators to ask questions that will inform the field as a whole.

New approaches to evaluating community change challenge traditional roles and make new capacities necessary.

Evaluations that draw on theories of change and promote continuous learning have created new challenges and new capacities for community-change endeavors. Evaluators are more engaged with initiatives at the outset than in the past, which can be useful; but as they facilitate initiatives' efforts to define outcomes, activities, and pathways of change, the line between evaluation and technical assistance blurs. They are left in the awkward position of evaluating something they have helped to create.

Despite the new roles, tension remains between evaluators and those being evaluated. Because evaluation is almost always commissioned and paid for by funders, they are inevitably the evaluators' primary constituents. This relationship emphasizes the accountability dimension of evaluation, with predictable anxiety-provoking results. Still, practitioners express a desire to use the evaluation process as an entry point for honest discussions with funders about what is happening in the initiative. As one explained,

You have to tell the funders that this initiative or project involves risk and that you'll make mistakes. It's important to be honest. Tell them, 'We've discovered this problem, here's what we're doing about it, here's how you can help us.' Frame your plans as though it's an experiment and you want to test things out.

Few practitioners report such an open and mutually supportive relationship with their funders around evaluation, however. Instead, practitioners say they concentrate on reducing the "we vs. they" dynamic.

One strategy is to build evaluation capacity among CCI stakeholders within the neighborhood. It is possible to include residents, program staff, and other stakeholders as active participants in planning and managing the evaluation process. When community members become informed consumers of evaluation, they become able to direct the course of the evaluation so it better meets their needs, they feel more powerful, and the products of evaluation become more useful. As one resident recalled,

We had a couple of evaluation teams that we were disappointed with. Then we started learning about what we wanted to know and so we were better situated to know what we wanted and choose the evaluator. We were able to go back to the evaluator and tell her that she left certain things out. We withheld the final payment. But we had to develop the capacity ourselves.

Locating data collection and analysis functions within the community also improves the planning process. Too often, data about the neighborhood are locked within government agencies or researchers' computers. The more a community knows about its own circumstances, the more informed planning and decision making can be.

KNOWLEDGE DEVELOPMENT

A laudable feature of many CCIs is the emphasis they place on evaluation and learning. Some have structured evaluations so that the initiatives themselves become a venue for asking and answering pressing questions about how to promote social change. Some have also built in opportunities to share early lessons and challenges with peers and other interested parties.

These and other elements compose what some people call "a learning community" which, if structured properly, can be an enormous support to neighborhood organizations and other agents of social change. But an even more deliberate effort to extract practical lessons from ongoing community-change efforts, and to link them with recent scholarship on the issues and effects of neighborhood change, would help suggest new, better theories and strategies for community change.

Future community-change ventures can help build such a knowledge base by developing clearer guidance on the goals of community change, the principles that guide action, effective implementation strategies, and the roles that all participants play in the process. The following areas of work need special attention.

Better theories of change would clearly express the links between activities and outcomes, including how stakeholders will implement strategies.

Most comprehensive community initiatives have been guided not by clearly articulated theories of change but by broad principles of action, based on convictions about the nature of communities and the origins and consequences of poverty. Theories about the causes of and possible responses to poverty and neighborhood change have tended to focus either on micro-level influences (the impact of individual behavior) or macro-level influences (broad structural changes in the economic, social, and political context).

CCIs focus on the mediating processes that can operate between the micro and macro levels. They recognize that individuals are embedded in networks of relationships through which they receive resources, information, and aid. Community-change efforts try to address the relationships among individual behavior, neighborhood social structure, and the community overall by simultaneously enhancing the capacities of residents and community organizations and reconnecting neighborhoods to external resources. But the assumptions people make about how community-change efforts will actually achieve these goals are murky. In the words of one CCI director,

> *My assessment is that much of the CCI work has been opportunistic. We talk about a field, we talk about theories of change, but we don't really have them. There are a lot of us out there*

experimenting in various ways, trying to find our way in the dark. I'd call where we are: "moving toward a theory of change."

It is possible to specify the components of theories of change and the relationships among them, even for the complex and multi-faceted community change efforts. "Theory," in our context, is not abstract; it is a concrete statement of plausible, testable pathways of change that can both guide actions and explain their impact. In this way, a theory of change provides a roadmap for action and a frame-work to chart and monitor progress over time. Better-articulated the-ories of change would support community-change efforts by specifying how various stakeholders, working at specific points of intervention, will pursue goals at different levels of the ecology of change.

Theories of practice must do a better job of translating princi-ples into actions, influencing communities' and organizations' capacity for change, and addressing the structural factors that affect residents and neighborhoods.

The principles of community, comprehensiveness, participation, col-laboration, democracy, empowerment, and capacity building have served community-change initiatives well, in some ways. They have drawn attention and sometimes significant resources to poor neigh-borhoods. They have shifted the focus from categorical, remedial approaches to holistic, asset-based, developmental ones. The process of applying the principles has driven community revitalization efforts to produce real outcomes—for businesses, jobs, housing, services—and vital connections among organizations and individuals. And it has strengthened the support structures—consultants and intermedi-ary organizations, training centers and curricula, funders, and research organizations—that facilitate and inform the work of practi-tioners across the nation.

These broad principles have provided less guidance for action than people need, however. Moreover, the principles sometimes com-pete for dominance, creating fundamental tensions in the approaches that implementers take. The fact that communities are embedded in a context of historical structures, economic and political factors, cultural assumptions, social dynamics, and organizational relation-ships makes community building a complicated thing to translate into practice. The strategies that people have used to produce better communities—such as mobilizing residents, developing new leaders, implementing good practices from other programs, building effective organizations, and collaborating around shared interests—are extremely difficult to implement well. Each step along the path spawns new challenges as various participants and institutions exert their influence and roles and relationships change.

These circumstances raise the following types of questions, as yet unanswered: How should we translate community-building principles into practice? How can we gauge capacity for change and influence it? How should we deal with major external, structural factors? How can we address the dynamic nature of the change process?

Armed with better theories, participants in community change need to test new strategies, learn from them, and disseminate their results.

Knowledge development supports community change by strengthening its building blocks—theories of change and practice—and augmenting them with improved research and dissemination. Better research supports, for example, might include syntheses of existing knowledge and efforts to gain new knowledge from applied and basic research. Dissemination supports would make information accessible to many audiences and help them use the information effectively.

Creation of a learning community would provide a structure for gaining and applying knowledge about achieving results for individuals, families, and communities. As one representative of an intermediary organization noted,

> *Capacity is so essential and it has to be built. But we don't have the means of capturing experience [and] transferring it from one place to another. . . . So, for everyone, it's just sort of 'catch as catch can.' And we're all drawing on the same few folks and often they're consultants. So sometimes their information is proprietary, but in any case it's not institutionalized anywhere. The flip side of capacity building is the helping environment, and we need to develop a 'helping infrastructure.'*

Useful knowledge development activities might produce the following products:

❖ A thorough review, synthesis, and assessment of current knowledge

❖ New knowledge about the processes of community change, based on empirical evidence from several communities (for example, using a panel study)

❖ Local infrastructures for collecting and sharing information on neighborhood circumstances and dynamics, including tools and resources for collecting and using data and for making administrative data easier to share and manipulate

❖ Pragmatic, systematic, diagnostic evaluations of specific community-change efforts, including comparative case studies that link such evaluations to one another

❖ Strategies for sharing information with diverse stakeholders (policymakers, funders, program managers and staff, members of governing bodies, program clients, and community residents) that respond to the audiences' needs and interests and engage them in developing questions and research approaches, identifying data sources, and interpreting findings

❖ Well-structured demonstrations of community change that attempt to measure outcomes, gauge the social effects of community building, and establish causes and effects

OUR FRAMEWORK FOR COMMUNITY CHANGE IN THIS CHAPTER MOVED beyond neighborhood boundaries to the resources and supports found in external organizations. As our thinking expanded, so did the potential for innovative new directions of work. That trend continues as we turn to the fourth level in our ecology of change: entities that focus on the policies and practices of external power structures.

VI.

STRENGTHENING THE CONNECTIONS BETWEEN COMMUNITIES AND EXTERNAL RESOURCES

T HE CONCENTRATION OF POOR PEOPLE—ESPECIALLY POOR people of color—in urban pockets of poverty did not occur by chance in this country, or solely as the result of choices made by residents of those communities. The racial and economic isolation, poverty concentration, and political disempowerment that characterize America's poor communities are largely the result of identifiable policies and practices embedded in public and private systems and in our society's power structures—factors that would exist even without a community-change agenda. They contribute to the persistently poor social and economic outcomes experienced in the neighborhoods that are the targets of community-change efforts, and they reinforce segregation by race and class.

This suggests that community-building solutions must understand how these systems, rules, and structures affect poor neighborhoods, and then make them work better by tapping into the resources of outside institutions and influencing their actions. That observation raises serious questions, however:

How well do community-change efforts incorporate historical and structural phenomena into the solutions they develop? Does the very nature of community-based change lead to a bias toward "local" issues and away from overarching, structural ones? Is it possible to integrate the work done by community members on their own behalf, within neighborhoods, with efforts to influence external players—or do the demands of working within communities preclude or limit such activities? Are the limitations imposed by external funding sources, systems, economic dynamics, and public policies so forbidding that neighborhood improvement is the best that we can hope for? Will the political and funding climate tolerate this type of work, which is more politically oriented than in the past? What range of institutions and alliances do we need to tackle these issues?

This chapter argues that participants in community building need to reinvigorate their approach to community change so that it addresses the external relationships and structural factors operating outside communities. Our discussion focuses especially on the inherent issues and tensions of four key activities: *broadening the analysis of the problem, finding powerful allies, working with the public and private sectors, and re-examining the assumptions and biases embedded in the community-building approach.*

BROADENING THE ANALYSIS OF THE PROBLEM

The principle of community building has several philosophical underpinnings that emphasize the power of "place" and the assets of neighborhood residents. Looking back at the way community-based initiatives unfolded and the evidence of what they have and have not achieved, a fundamental tension becomes clear. In its most extreme characterization, the tension is this: While focusing inward on internal community dynamics and capacities, many community change advocates have not sufficiently addressed external structures, which can enhance or constrain their success. As one community organizer said, "The neighborhood is the heart of our work. It's the beginning and the end." A policymaker responded, "The irony is that we're missing the big things because we've seen neighborhood as the heart of our work. You're not going to fix things just by what you do inside the four corners of low-income neighborhoods."

On one hand, practitioners and funders believe in the power of poor people in poor communities to change their environment and take control of their own destinies. They laud residents' abilities as leaders, and they recognize the strengths and capacities residents develop as participants in community change. Yet in practice, by focusing on neighborhood residents' capacity for change, many community-building efforts have implicitly diminished, underestimated, or simply been unable to influence the power of external institutions, public policies, and private market dynamics.

Forward-looking participants in community change are looking for a new way to frame their work that captures the critical importance of addressing external issues, even as they continue to expand and deepen capacity-building efforts within their communities. They agree, as one person said, that "framing the problem really matters. If it is framed as internal, that leads to one set of actions; but if it is framed differently, it may lead to a very different set of priorities entirely." Acknowledging the power of the policy environment, many conclude that an internal focus is a losing strategy for even the most exemplary practitioners. They argue for a new approach that links policy, politics, and place on a metropolitan level around the goal of expanding opportunities for poor people. Observed one practitioner, "If you just do neighborhoods, all you've done is create an oasis in the desert." Agreed an evaluator:

> The things that are changing through efforts focused within communities are the smaller things. . . . We're not getting at power, income redistribution, system change, etc. Do we believe that initiatives that don't address these external issues make real changes for kids and families? My sense is yes—but only at the margins.

Essentially, this "localism" leaves prevailing economic and political paradigms unchallenged and approaches urban poverty as a problem for neighborhoods and their residents. Critics suggest that, instead of adding an additional set of approaches and strategies to an aging toolbox in need of innovation, CCIs seemed to displace, reinterpret, or silence an older consciousness about the structure of poverty, racism, and the alignments of power that maintain the status quo. As the director of an intermediary organization noted:

> We can make substantial gains [in moving people out of poverty], but we've essentially conceded to a system that will constantly reproduce it. The redistribution we're talking about is public aid dollars, not the structural redistribution of wealth.

"We are guilty of having a sophisticated comprehensive analysis but acting only at the community level . . . I am not saying we should forget working at the community level. It is absolutely necessary, but not sufficient."

—Funder

Practitioners, scholars, policymakers and residents can point to several issues that need to be re-infused into the analysis of the problem. Problems with economic development and housing policies are particularly resonant. For example:

❖ Public policies and investments promoted the movement of middle-class workers and jobs to the suburbs and left poor people of color isolated in inner-city neighborhoods. As the regional and national economies shifted from manufacturing to service and technology, employment opportunities became more mobile, the labor market split into high- and low-wage sectors, and residents of poor communities were left behind.

❖ Housing policies exacerbated the problem. Public housing, intended as a temporary support for people in economic crisis, became in many places permanent housing for the persistently poor due to processes for selecting tenants, a lack of adequate services, discriminatory site-selection policies, the construction of high-density developments, and isolation from surrounding communities. Today, exclusionary zoning practices often preclude subsidized housing in the suburbs or raise the cost of building suburban housing to prohibitive levels. Property tax policies discourage economic integration in the suburbs and make mixed-income communities hard to create or maintain in cities.

These and similar issues, fueled by powerful political forces that are extremely difficult to budge, shape the context within which CCIs operate. In the words of one African-American researcher,

> These things did not happen by chance. Those distressed neighborhoods exist because of policies, procedures, and programs that have been in place in powerful neighborhoods. The zoning laws, the building codes ... an entire infrastructure was built in the first half of the 20th century to create the type of segregation that meant that the communities that white people grew up in could only exist because of the type of communities that I grew up in. Now, the problem with all of this is that you can't change the conditions in that neighborhood without restructuring the whole paradigm. There are forces that profit a segment of this society, and until equal or superior forces come to check that group we're not going to have the kind of change we seek.

The challenge is not to give up the local-level work but to do a better job of balancing and aligning the two levels. One leader in the field of community change, who has worked both in government and in communities, explained:

> It's a balance issue—working on the internal and working on the external. The question is, how much of each? Is it roughly half and half? Eighty-twenty? Ninety-ten? Obviously, it matters what community you're talking about, but how do you decide? We've gotten much better at the internal. The two feed each other in important ways, and there's a tremendous amount of middle ground that we have to work on.

To find that balance, leaders of change in poor neighborhoods need to do two things. First, they must identify the causes of the problems they are experiencing, in the broadest possible way. That means stopping for a moment to consider the historical, institutional, and structural origins of problems. If people begin and end their analysis within the community, they may miss important contextual factors that affect everything they do. As one person commented, "If your 'hammer' is a CCI, then the only 'nails' that you tend to see are the things that a CCI has control over."

The second step is to identify sources of power outside the neighborhood that can be tapped or influenced to help the community. Again, the challenge here is to cast the net wide, well beyond traditional philanthropies or public programs, to include various levels of government and various types of policies as well as the role of the private sector.

Armed with the results of those activities, participants in community-change efforts can develop strategies for addressing fundamental issues. Judging from the experiences of recent CCIs and other endeavors, those strategies are likely to include finding powerful allies, working with the public and private sectors in new ways, and re-examining the assumptions and biases that are embedded in community building.

FINDING POWERFUL ALLIES

Although CCIs and other community-building ventures should recognize the *need* to engage forces outside their communities, they don't have to lead engagement efforts themselves. CCIs do not have the capacity or the power base for that responsibility. In the words of one observer,

> We are right in saying that you can't solve the problems in poor neighborhoods without addressing the range of structural issues that are reproducing and have reinforced and maintained those problems. But, in my mind, that's not necessarily the same thing as saying that CCIs are the best vehicles for addressing those structural issues. There are strategic allies that they could and should connect with. There's probably a division of labor in the broader context that CCIs could coordinate and leverage. You don't have to take on more, you have to find partners to fight the fight. We have to think about coalitions, finding out who's working on these issues and connecting the community voices to those discussions.

The people interviewed for this book offered the following observations about what those "strategic alliances" might look like.

Alliances with national, state, and local policy groups that advocate for disadvantaged groups give community-change initiatives access to expertise and influence in the policy world.
The challenge for CCIs and other community-based groups lies in knowing how to reach out and build those alliances. Policy groups vary in their focus and strategies; some address specific populations, such as children, the elderly, or people of color, while others focus on topics, such as housing or transportation. Some concentrate on lobbying for money, while others pursue systemic change through the legal system.

It is unlikely that there will ever be a policy organization equipped to take on the full range of issues encompassed by a comprehensive community-change agenda. Therefore, alliances need to form across many different vehicles for change. For example, one avenue of work might revolve around policies, such as the housing mortgage tax deduction, which are broad and "non-targeted" but benefit the upper and middle classes more than low-income people. Here, alliances with national housing advocacy groups make sense. Other work might focus on key moments in the legislative cycle, such as reauthorization of welfare or of the Community Reinvestment Act. Or, there might be policy trends that offer opportunities for advocacy. One policy organization, for instance, has picked up on the issue of regionalism:

> We are focused on those situations that can better connect poor communities with opportunities throughout the region. That has to do with workforce development policy, opportunities for wealth creation in poor communities, the spatial mismatch between housing and jobs, transportation, and a whole range of issues that disconnect poor communities from opportunity.

Coalitions across neighborhoods can expand the base and, consequently, the influence of political constituents.
In one good example, a community group joined with people in two other neighborhoods to establish a leadership institute that taught residents how to influence policy at the city and state levels. "It was important to team with other communities in order to lobby and advocate—for example, with the school board," a practitioner recalled. Other practitioners, cognizant of the suburbs' influence on

state legislatures, are considering connections with allies outside their neighborhoods, such as rural districts that are similarly poor but have more voting power.

Alliances across neighborhoods can become more powerful by including connections to middle-class communities as well as other poor neighborhoods, practitioners note. "If you only organize poor communities then you will largely be limited to federal funds, and they tend to come with more strings attached," one person observed. His coalition paired people from rich and poor neighborhoods:

> *When the representatives from economically secure (and power-ful) neighborhoods went before city council, they would natu-rally act as advocates for poor communities as well. This was also a way for wealthier communities to develop a knowledge of poor ones—these were areas they would never have gone into otherwise.*

Activities that mobilize residents' political power and use it to influence policy discussions increase the pressure on political forces outside the community.

The problems of poor neighborhoods are as much political as they are technical. That fact suggests the need for a new "politics" of community building—one with explicit strategies for exerting pressure on the people and institutions who do not naturally serve the interests of disadvantaged people. In the words of one practitioner, "We thought they would want to change once they saw our point of view, but big institutions don't change their business just because they like you. You've got to bring your own power to the partnership, or it won't work. Don't expect them to give it to you."

"Our focus has been on organizing people on the neighborhood level. That is too small to get to the systems-change agenda, because the tough part is trying to get all the players on the local level together. The systems themselves are subject to political whim. So while you are organizing locally, the big system continues to do its own thing."

—Resident

Participating in the political arena can lead to examination of and (sometimes) conflict around fundamental ideological issues. As a former public official observed,

> *If we want to have the honest conversation about how do something for poor neighborhoods, we are actually engaging on the most controversial aspect of American poverty. We have to be clear about why those neighborhoods got into such a serious state of distress. And then we have to work our way from that explanation to what the strategies for change are that aren't just about trying to "fix those people" by telling them to pull up their socks and be responsible for themselves.*

Many practitioners and even some funders now call for a more explicit political agenda, both to put pressure on the public and private sectors and out of a core commitment to reaching and activating residents. As one practitioner said, "If community building isn't oriented toward a political agenda, why would we do it? For me, civic engagement is necessarily directed toward policy change."

The new emphasis on politics occurs at the most basic level of neighborhood work, on issues that directly affect children and families. It involves "pressure organizing, coalition building, and collaborative negotiation," in the words of one executive director. The political side of community building means mobilizing residents' political power around neighborhood concerns, for example, and activating voters. A CDC that targeted voter apathy claimed to have doubled the turnout in precincts where it worked and then turned its attention to holding the newly elected representatives accountable to the community. Others have mobilized parents to plan school reform and influence local school boards. "The small boats move the freighters," observed a board member of one such organization. "[Our work] helped the mayor by providing political cover. It also contributed to better involvement of parents and the community."

> **"The power of ideas is not enough. The ideas need to be delivered to the group that can deliver the phone calls. There is a need to create communities of interest. . . . Whatever process you use, you have to mobilize your constituency."**
>
> **—CCI Director**

The development of political consciousness does not necessarily entail large-scale movements or electoral activities. Efforts to build political connections encompass a range of organizing styles.

Community organizing runs the gamut from "hell raising" to "relationship building." Observers suggest the need for both ends of the spectrum:

> *I feel like we keep shifting back and forth between confrontation-style organizing and consensus-style organizing. On the ground, there needs to be a blend if we're smart. I think it's more about how to be proficient at both—being able to talk like equals to the corporate heads and the lieutenant governor as well as to be able to talk tough to them.*

Some practitioners take a pragmatic approach; they will work with anyone, at any level of the political system, who can help them address local concerns. Others look for simple, practical ways to assert their power. In the words of a technical assistance provider,

> *When I think about power, I think about communities that can get a prison located in their community for economic development, or a water processing plant, or a one-stop job center located. If a community can purposely do those things—sometimes it's organizing, sometimes it's good leverage politics. Power is not necessarily a movement. It can be very grounded and incremental.*

The ability to use information strategically is as important as policy acumen and an agenda for change.

Knowledge about the nuances of power and policy making helps community stakeholders organize, understand, and prepare for policy changes. Current community-building efforts are beginning to track and share information about broad issues at the state and local levels, such as transportation and land use. A representative of an intermediary organization described the dramatic effect that a little bit of information can have:

> *A number of years ago the IAF [Industrial Areas Foundation] had training for its organizers. One session was a famous social scientist talking about poverty concentration and the other was on land policy and water policy in Texas . . . I had absolutely no*

interest in water policy in Texas but suddenly all this stuff I'd seen made sense. It helped me understand politics and power there, how and why money is appropriated, who votes on what sides, who finances the campaign.

Communities that lack capacity for gathering and analyzing such information are forming connections with universities and statewide organizations to expand their reach. In one community, for instance, university students have worked with residents to understand trends in gentrification and to help them find ways to address the problem. There are many other examples of this type of work.

Practitioners also are beginning to think strategically about the information that decision makers get about their communities, and they are finding ways to shape the public dialogue. For example, when race-based assumptions began to drive discussions about welfare reform in a state legislature dominated by suburban interests, a community organization produced information that recast the discourse:

> **"The way we organize sometimes can be self-defeating if we lose the importance of educating and giving the proper information to our constituencies so they become knowledgeable. . . . We shouldn't just try to turn them out on buses, we should make sure they understand more."**
>
> **—Resident**

Most of what was done was based on the premise that benefits were going to the black communities in the city, which was not true. If you don't show that, then the legislators create policies that effect [too little] change . . . because they don't see it as being about their constituencies. What resulted was that we had to bring in a white lady to testify. . . . We had to take someone from their local area and from the suburban area and get them to tell their story, and then we reinforced it with data.

WORKING WITH THE PUBLIC SECTOR

Community-building efforts have come of age at a time when ideas about government responsibility for developing, testing, and replicating model programs are changing. People can no longer assume that the public sector will provide money for successful approaches. Noted a practitioner:

> *We need a more deliberate and fact-based strategy for engaging the public sector, from the beginning. We should not just have a presumption that the public sector will take over. . . . We used to believe that the 'model and transfer' thing worked, but it doesn't. It is pretty hard to find an example of where that actually happened.*

At the same time, many practitioners and funders suggest that initiatives have not been resourceful enough in pursuing public money. "If the money being spent by public service agencies could be redirected, there'd be enough money to do everything we're trying to do at the neighborhood level," says the director of an intermediary organization. "That is where long-term sustainability exists—in redirecting the streams of funding."

Public officials say that government wants to join with private and nonprofit supporters of communities, and that the timing is ripe. As one former federal official described,

> *There's a whole range of government trends that are coming together to give communities and CCI types of interventions prominence. There's the search for efficiency in things like service integration. Then there's devolution, where the feds were told that the states know better, and state were told that the local government knows better, and local government is told that communities know better. And so all of this seems to me to be coming together and giving communities a chance to play with government in a different way.*

The challenge is to figure out how to make the relationship work effectively, in part because the relationship between community-building initiatives and government is a tricky one—part collaboration, part supplication, and part a quest for reform. Experienced participants in publicly funded community building offer the following observations as guidance.

Community organizations need a better sense of the public funding streams that come into their neighborhoods.

Very few community-level actors have a clear sense of the amount and types of government money that flows into their neighborhoods. As one person noted,

> You have to know how to do an inventory and count the money coming into the neighborhood or develop an alliance with somebody to help you do it. We have a strategic agenda for the $300,000 in foundation grant money but there's maybe $10 million in public money that we can't even count. We need to find out how much money is coming in in welfare, in police, fire, education, and so on.

Getting a full picture of funding streams is a first step in understanding where the opportunities for increases or changes are likely to be. But practitioners say it is very difficult to get the information, because each funding stream is organized and directed differently. "It's not just apples and oranges, it's a whole fruit salad," said one practitioner. Representatives of community organizations further suggest that government workers have little incentive to disclose the information, because it would give outsiders tools for negotiating and pressuring the system. Said one,

> In my city, which is pretty small, there's about $25 million in Community Development Block Grant funds, and probably less than 10 percent are really spent on ways to impact neighborhoods. If you spend any time at city hall, you become amazed at how poorly those dollars are spent and how they get spent in ways that don't get to the neighborhoods. So you've really got to know what's there and how to access it.

Nonetheless, financial experts have helped people in some communities put information into the hands of residents so they could hold the public sector accountable for investments. In one neighborhood, a CCI convened 20 residents for a year-long process of assessing organizational effectiveness, using a standard set of questions and a framework for analyzing responses. That process produced an informed watchdog group that could exert pressure when organizations outside the neighborhood, such as the community college or health department, failed to meet community needs.

Using financial information to enforce accountability is especially important in low-income communities that receive substantial government resources "on behalf of the community" without formal accountability requirements.

Engaging effectively with the public sector means looking beyond financing to broad policy issues that affect poor communities.

Many public policies that have a significant impact on neighborhood circumstances seem distant to people who are working to change communities, but in fact community members can engage local policymaking institutions—including workforce investment boards, economic development authorities, business improvement districts, school boards, and transportation authorities—around a variety of issues.

Community groups might target specific agencies, such as a police department's "stop and frisk" policies, which affect communities of color much more than other neighborhoods. Or they might analyze a variety of public policies and practices that add up to a "report card" for the local government, as one former public official suggested:

> *Are they looking at their purchasing power? Are they looking at who they are and where they live? Are they looking at where they invest their cash reserves? Is the local government using its relationship with the cable TV company to address the digital divide? There's a whole host of things that could be itemized clearly enough that CCIs could have a much richer conversation with local government. All we've ever asked them for is a little piece of Community Development Block Grant money. We've never thought about any of those other things.*

Even extremely specific policies offer opportunities to exert community pressure. For example, when a city council considers granting a tax abatement to a company, community participants might negotiate to make livable wages or hiring agreements a precondition.

Local government should figure much more prominently in community-change initiatives.

The former government officials interviewed for this book expressed surprise that CCIs had not developed better methods for working with local government. "Local government has an inevitable role in local change enterprises. It may be a target for action or a full leader in community level work, but it is never irrelevant," one stated. Local government not only is the source of much public money, it also has broader powers and responsibilities that affect communities. It is the maker, interpreter, or enforcer of rules governing how federal and state programs are implemented, from decentralization mandates to local purchasing policies to the blending of funding streams. Local government also is an information conduit between communities and outside entities.

Although the involvement of top city officials often boosts community change initiatives, it does not always translate into long-term change. Political rivalries, turnover in leadership, and bureaucracy can disrupt the community-building process.

Mayors and other city officials have taken active roles in neighborhood revitalization, bringing resources, legitimacy, and visibility. But these political connections are not without risk. Constituencies can become alienated, newly elected officials frequently abandon their predecessors' projects, and deeply embedded bureaucratic interests may block action.

Moreover, the senior administrators who support community building are not the people charged with carrying out public policies on the ground. "We discovered that getting the policy right wasn't enough," recalled one public official. "So we set up a middle management training system to be able to sustain the initiatives on the execution side. . . . If you focus just on the state capital then you miss the people who do the transactions."

WORKING WITH THE PRIVATE SECTOR

Distressed communities need the deep pockets of the private sector to help them achieve their ambitious goals for community change. But private-sector connections are an unmined resource for most community-change initiatives. As a longtime practitioner observed, "[People] look to the government, nonprofits, or the community for resources. They have got to get unsentimental about who does what and stop being naïve about how the economy works." Community-change ventures that have used or considered private-sector resources offer the following observations.

The greatest challenge is to connect with mainstream capital markets in ways that do not disrupt the community.

For several years, people have discussed the advantages of investing in inner-city neighborhoods. With their access to transportation, physical infrastructure, and historic appeal, poor inner-city neighborhoods can be attractive investment sites. Thus corporations that are unlikely to give money for nonprofit activities might find reasons for more intensive investments in poor communities. In the words of an experienced technical assistance provider, "The fate of regions and low-income communities is tied up with the new economy. At the community level, we need to find and reduce the hidden costs of doing business so that we can get businesses to harness their resources to the benefit of the community."

Experience shows that there are risks with this strategy, however. As a former public official noted,

> I think many of us think that income diversification in a neighborhood is a good thing. But obviously the unacceptable price that you could end up paying is complete displacement of the population; the very people you want to heal are driven away. How do we accomplish [progress] in a way that doesn't hurt people?

In some areas, it is possible to tap into private-sector resources and still maintain community control over their use. As a community development expert explained,

> We've been doing our own financing with community development organizations for over 20 years now. We've sometimes done it quite well. But what we have now is a 'capital connection' problem. It's not a capital 'gap,' it's connecting to what's out there. There has been some infrastructure built but that's where the work needs to take place now. We have the track record of

leveraging financing for communities but there's a lot more that could be done.

People who think creatively about funding community change can find support from unconventional sources.

There are many sources of money that are not necessarily obvious to community groups and other local engines of community change. Some local organizations report success in obtaining private capital for community trust funds, construction, and home mortgages. Some use eminent domain authority to support affordable housing and economic development. Private companies may also divert a portion of the funds in their investment portfolios for social purposes. For example, insurance companies interested in investing some portion of their funds in safe securities have agreed to give up a few points on their earnings to help with endowments of historically black colleges. There have been examples of credit union groups encouraging mainstream credit unions to put some of their money into an investment pool and agreeing that a small proportion of the earnings will go to communities. Community-building initiatives can also tap people who have spent their careers in the corporate world for knowledge about funding streams, innovative financing tools, and hidden market opportunities.

It isn't easy to ensure corporate accountability to neighborhoods, but some communities report successes.

Corporations receive many public subsidies and loans, and some grassroots groups have drawn corporations into community-building activities by holding them accountable for these privileges. Approaches include campaigns for: livable wages and benefits, community hiring goals and agreements, job training and retention services, improved local environmental standards, and retail services that meet community needs.

But the battle is an uphill one. As one community planner reported,

In the poorest neighborhood in my city there are more than 10,000 jobs. And there are almost 50,000 jobs within walking distance of the neighborhood. The problem is that the people who live in the neighborhood are not connected to those jobs. Sixty percent of the people who work in the factories and other

businesses are from the suburbs and 35 percent live in other,
middle income neighborhoods in the city. The people in the local
neighborhoods—who are poor!—get only 5 percent of the jobs.
I don't yet know why because we've just discovered this but we're
going to find out what's keeping the people in these neighbor-
hoods from accessing the jobs.

Some people fear that the moment to push for greater corporate
accountability peaked in the late 1990s when the labor market was
tight. "That would have been the time to negotiate over the quality of
jobs and the benefits and security that came with the jobs," one analyst said. "We let them keep the agenda focused on 'soft skills' rather
than taking up questions like the composition of the work investment
boards which are still all corporate."

Poor communities are losing out in the rapid transformations of the private sector.

Corporations are going through many changes that have dramatic
effects on low-wage workers and low-income communities. They are
downsizing, increasing their numbers of contractors, cutting benefits,
and moving overseas. As an analyst explained,

One of the great paradoxes of modern advanced capitalism is
that there has been a separation of ownership from manage-
ment. The fact is that the corporation is much more concerned
about the stock price on any given day than in what's going on
the local community. So, how can we put pressure on these com-
panies for investments in communities that they don't even see?
It used to be that the local bank had an owner or managers who
had some link to the local community. But if the headquarters is
now in Germany, how do you get the bank to focus on your com-
munity's needs? The fear of reprisals is pretty remote.

Globalization, revolutions in information technology, and shifting demographics are all trends that are likely to benefit those with
access to power and influence at the expense of the poor and politically weak. Thus it is vitally important for low-income communities
and their supporters to understand how to reduce the negative consequences of globalization and maximize the positive ones.

RE-EXAMINING THE ASSUMPTIONS AND BIASES EMBEDDED IN THE COMMUNITY-BUILDING APPROACH

Although practitioners and funders of community building generally have deep experience with the historical, structural, and racial constraints imposed on poor people by mainstream society, most have limited their focus to the local neighborhood. They view it as both the starting point and the fundamental core of community change. Why? There are several possible explanations, all of which represent ongoing tensions in the community-building arena.

Some observers defend the core assumptions behind recent community-change efforts but say the political climate narrowed the range of possible strategies for change.

The social justice and democracy movements of the 1960s and 1970s were powerful forces behind the proliferation of CDCs and other local change efforts of the time. In those years, political empowerment, grassroots participation, and institutional change emerged as important local capacity issues. But the civil rights consciousness that infused community revitalization theory and practice in the beginning—especially the sense that chronic disadvantages for minority groups were structural and institutional problems—lost ground to the resurgent individualism of the "Reagan revival" during the 1980s.

Some observers believe that the resulting funding climate constrained the activities of change agents. Foundations, too, retreated from "political" funding, and progressive values adopted a more communitarian outlook. When it came time to translate the assumptions into action, critics suggest, funders would not support fundamental social change or tackle the really tough political and structural issues of power, access, and race faced by poor communities. "If you push that hard for real revolutionary change, the status quo will squash you," an evaluator said. Some practitioners now wonder whether foundations can ever truly be in the vanguard of democratic social change since they are, after all, the direct by-products of corporate power and historical privilege.

Community-change efforts have promoted collaboration across racial and cultural lines but have not taken the lead in advocating for responses to the fact that all levels of the political economy sort Americans by race—institutionally, geographically, and psychologically.

Many residents and frontline practitioners describe the problems of poor, inner-city communities in ways that reflect a structural analysis of racism. These observers highlight assumptions, practices, and institutional behaviors that consistently give poor people of color too few of society's benefits and too many of society's punishments. They recognize that entrenched white privilege and minority stereotyping in major institutions continually undermine individual and local community gains, as revealed by the policies and practices of public education, housing, employment, transportation, law enforcement, and other social institutions. They suggest that attention to race necessarily leads to a more externally oriented strategy for rectifying race-related disparities in urban outcomes, a strategy that addresses institutional and systemic issues. This knowledge does not carry over into the design of community-change ventures, however. As one community activist suggested:

> *Most initiatives to change things in neighborhood settings have a good analysis of symptoms. But failure is more likely when looking at symptoms rather than the root cause of problems, which is white privilege and other structural advantages and disadvantages. Many communities don't have a chance to do that analysis at the local level. Communities need to be able to understand how certain forms of privilege—political, social, or economic—are working in a particular place at a particular point in time.*

Many observers believe that the focus on developing broad social relationships, networks, partnerships, and collaborations in communities failed to address issues of social justice, which are firmly rooted in policies and arrangements of power.

Many participants in community change have operated under the assumption that the work of reinforcing social connections could rebuild the fabric of a community and lead to other broader positive changes. Their work generally focused on building trust and understanding among stakeholders, through collaboration and consensus. While that dimension of the work continues to be important, there is some concern that it underestimates the crucial work of "politicizing" communities so they can tackle tough political and policy issues. The result, as one participant said, is that communities "have been collaborated to death and what do we have to show for it? I don't see that much has changed on their side."

> "Unless there's a radical shift in the unjust systems in our city, what we do isn't a drop in the bucket. To put all our efforts into community building takes the fire out of efforts to push the systems of justice. Community building isn't the solution to the long-term injustice of the systems. It's not enough. We siphon off the fire in the belly into 'just' community building."
>
> **—CDC Director**

Some analysts believe that the commitment to place-based approaches underestimated the dynamic nature of communities. Some critics say that community building treats people and communities as fixed and unchanging, while in reality communities are dynamic. Most Americans move frequently, and most jobs are located outside workers' neighborhoods. Instead, they suggest, community-change efforts should enable residents to choose where they live so they can have better access to jobs. As the representative of an intermediary organization said,

> *If we're building community, for individuals in these neighborhoods, a part of it may be about them leaving: the pattern of upward mobility leading to moving to a better place. Why should we expect the residents of low-income communities to have different aspirations from those of us who work in these communities and don't live there?*

CCIs AND OTHER COMMUNITY-CHANGE EFFORTS HAVE ENGAGED ONLY sporadically and superficially in efforts to make policies, power structures, and other influences outside their neighborhoods work on behalf of poor communities. As this chapter suggests, however, opportunities do exist to overcome, shape, or exploit those elements. Change can happen if people think broadly, act more politically and proactively than in the past, and form nontraditional alliances across sectors. Those obligations should therefore be on every current agenda for comprehensive community building.

CONCLUSION

A Call to Action

T HE LAST DECADE OF WORK BY CCIS AND RELATED COMMUNITY-
change efforts suggest that these endeavors have considerable
potential but also significant limitations. Comprehensive
community initiatives have made great strides in identifying the many
moving parts that have to come together to achieve change and in
understanding the principles that should guide the work. But they
have underestimated how difficult it is to implement complex community-change strategies and to acquire the capacities and resources
needed to make them work effectively. They have also overestimated
what community-based initiatives can be expected to do in order to
overcome poverty in distressed neighborhoods.

Our conclusion may sound disheartening to some. It will disap-
point that part of each of us that hopes for a clear and easy solution
to the problems of persistent poverty and social injustice. The stakeholders whose interviews and meetings shaped this book are not
disheartened, however. They are ready to take on the next phase of
work and to apply the lessons they have learned in significant,
sustained ways. In the words of one longtime observer, "We have

never had a full and faithful 'test' of the comprehensive community-building approach. Maybe we're finally ready."

The ecology of community change described in this book has four levels of action: by community residents; by community organizations; by support organizations; and by broad institutional, policy, or structural reform efforts. For social change to occur, participants at each level must have the internal capacity to be effective in their own domains of work and connections to actors at other levels that can reinforce and maximize their work. Based on the experience of CCIs and similar efforts over recent years, we can summarize the internal capacities and external connections of each level as follows.

Among *community residents*, years of experience in education, social services, employment, and other program areas have taught us a great deal about how to provide individuals with the skills and supports they need to do well in life. Lessons about the roles that individuals play in community change are more recent and less formed. We now understand that we need to improve individuals' ability to foster community change: they need to be brought into the work more deliberately and they need to become skilled leaders. Moreover, residents must connect with one another, as sources of social and material support and as mobilized partners in community change. The recent CCI experience has done well to identify leadership development, social capital, and community mobilization as important issues, but substantial progress remains to be made on improving how we do each.

Among *community institutions*, we have learned that most local organizations in poor communities are simply too weak to take on a comprehensive community-building agenda at a level that has potential for significant change. Organizations need straightforward, unglamorous capacity building within their staffs, boards, delivery and management systems, and monitoring and evaluation procedures.

If community institutions are to participate in far-reaching community change, they need to align their efforts with each other and with community members' interests. Here, the CCI experience has taught us a great deal about embarking on a community-wide vision and plan, creating governance and collaboration structures, and being responsive to all constituents on an ongoing basis. Although more work needs to be done, people have documented the lessons learned thus far and are applying them more effectively in successive iterations of community-change ventures.

Among *providers of support*, CCIs can count important successes. Early community-change efforts relied on technical assistance from external providers for such crucial activities as establishing and maintaining commitment to a vision for change; communicating among participants; collecting, analyzing, and presenting data; engaging in strategic planning, outreach, and organizing; and developing management systems and staff capacity. Funders, evaluators, intermediary organizations, independent consultants, and professional assistance providers all took responsibility for these supportive roles at different times in various initiatives.

Today, the structure of technical assistance is evolving away from externally driven, elite, and highly professionalized operations toward a strategy of helping people learn as they work. Evaluation designs are moving toward more meaningful blends of process documentation and outcomes tracking that can provide feedback to managers, constituents, and sponsors. Funders have developed more flexible ways of giving money, and they have assumed new roles and responsibilities for implementing the work. These positive changes certainly aren't as pervasive as they could be, and there is still a long way to go. But, in the context of CCIs, useful models for support have been tried, assessed, analyzed, and modified.

As we move beyond an initiative-oriented framework and think about community change more broadly, however, we need to think differently about supporting change. Supports must be available to a wider array of recipients and in ways that are more easily accessible. In all likelihood, this will mean further modifying practices—for example, by having funders provide more core support for capacity building and organizational development, by having research institutions partner directly with community organizations, and by developing technical expertise that links communities with innovative public- and private-sector financing. It will also require reforms within organizations that provide support so that they model the values and principles that community building encourages in ground-level institutions. And it may be necessary to develop new practices or institutions that can help participants in the change process share information and discover new ways to use resources, structures, and opportunities within and beyond the neighborhood.

It is at the level of engaging the *policies and practices of external resources* that CCIs have fallen most short. It is possible that their emphasis on "localism" steered them away from this type of work from the outset, but other factors also came into play. For the most part, poor communities are not well-situated to take the lead in building coalitions across neighborhoods and constituencies, an activity that requires significant effort and resources. Many people caution against placing too much responsibility for this work on the backs of community institutions. At the same time, we must keep in mind the inherent limitations of community-level work. Without sophisticated strategies for using structural, institutional, policy, and social levers for change, the work of CCIs will be merely palliative rather than transformative.

The question of how to strengthen this fourth level of action lies beyond the reach of community-change efforts. The goal of creating connections between communities and actors in the policy, research, and social action arena should be on everyone's agenda, however. Much of the national reform work that has important salience to distressed communities—from civil rights to trade policy—has operated without strong community-level engagement in recent years. There are some important exceptions (around regionalism or early child education, for example) that offer models for action and hope. But this work must be central to future action on the part of all of the participants in the ecology of change.

The next step is not to simply do more but to do the work better—to think more broadly and strategically, to chart better pathways through the conditions within and around poor communities, and to be sure that we embed learning opportunities as we go. Armed with a good understanding of ecology of community change and the strengths and weaknesses at each of its levels, we can begin to move beyond the limits of current community-change projects, programs, and initiatives.

APPENDIX I

MEMBERS OF THE
THE ASPEN INSTITUTE
ROUNDTABLE ON COMPREHENSIVE
COMMUNITY INITIATIVES

Harold Richman (Co-Chair)
  Hermon Dunlap Smith
    Professor
  The University of Chicago

Lisbeth B. Schorr (Co-Chair)
  Lecturer in Social Medicine
  Project on Effective
    Interventions at Harvard
    University

Michael Bailin
  President
  The Edna McConnell Clark
    Foundation

John Barros
  Executive Director
  Dudley Street Neighborhood
    Initiatives

Douglas Besharov
  Resident Scholar
  The American Enterprise
    Institute for Public Policy
    Research

Angela Blackwell
  President and CEO
  PolicyLink

Barbara B. Blum
  Senior Fellow in Child and
    Family Policy
  The National Center
    for Children in Poverty

Xavier de Souza Briggs
  Associate Professor
  John F. Kennedy School
    of Government
  Harvard University

Geoffrey Canada
President/CEO
Harlem Children's Zone

Gaetana D. Ebbole
Executive Director
Children's Services Council
of Palm Beach County

Peter Edelman
Professor of Law
Georgetown University
Law Center

Karen Fulbright-Anderson
Co-Director
Roundtable on
Comprehensive
Community Initiatives
The Aspen Institute

Sidney Gardner
President
Children and Family Futures

James Gibson
Senior Fellow
Center for the Study of
Social Policy

David Harris
Director of Regional Policy
and Florida Philanthropy
The John D. and Catherine T.
MacArthur Foundation

David Hornbeck
Consultant

Craig Howard
Vice President
Manpower Demonstration
Research Corporation

Paul Jellinek
Vice President
The Robert Wood Johnson
Foundation

Otis Johnson
Dean
The College of Liberal Arts
and Social Sciences
Savannah State University

Anne C. Kubisch
Co-Director
Roundtable on
Comprehensive
Community Initiatives
The Aspen Institute

Susan Lloyd
Director of Building
Community Capacity
The John D. and Catherine T.
MacArthur Foundation

Gayle McClure
Vice President of Programs
W. K. Kellogg Foundation

Anita Miller
Comprehensive Community
Revitalization Program

William A. Morrill
Senior Fellow
Caliber Associates

Robert O'Neill, Jr.
  President
  National Academy of Public
    Administration

Alvertha Bratton Penny
  Program Officer for Family
    and Community
    Development
  The William and Flora
    Hewlett Foundation

Terry Peterson
  Director
  Resource Network for
    Afterschool and
    Community Education

Ronald Register
  Consultant

Julius B. Richmond
  John D. MacArthur Professor
    of Health Policy, Emeritus
  Department of Social
    Medicine
  Harvard University

Mark Ridley-Thomas
  City Councilman, Eighth
    District
  City of Los Angeles

Charles Royer
  National Program Director
  Urban Health Initiative

Ann Segal
  The David and Lucile Packard
    Foundation

Ralph Smith
  Vice President
  The Annie E. Casey
    Foundation

Jeremy Travis
  Senior Fellow
  The Urban Institute

Gary Walker
  President
  Pubic/Private Ventures

Meeting Participants and Others Interviewed for *Voices from the Field II*

Terri Bailey
    The Piton Foundation

John Barros
    Dudley Street Neighborhood
    Initiatives

Diane Bell
    Empower Baltimore
    Management Corporation

Barbara Blum
    The National Center for
    Children In Poverty

Xavier de Souza Briggs
    John F. Kennedy School of
    Government
    Harvard University

Joseph Brooks
    PolicyLink

Thomas Burns
    OMG Center for
    Collaborative Learning

Benjamin Butler
    Community Development
    Associates, Inc.

Amanda Carney
    Local Initiatives Support
    Corporation

Chanelle Cooper
    Vision for Health

Dolores Santa Cruz
    East Valley Family YMCA

Maggie De Santis
Warren/Conner Development
Coalition

Gaetana D. Ebbole
Children's Services Council
of Palm Beach County

Peter Edelman
Georgetown University
Law Center

Rodney Fernandez
Cabrillo Economic
Development Corporation

Roxy Foster
Council for Civic
Parent Leadership

Abby Gamboa
Near Northside Partners
Council of Fort Worth

Sidney Gardner
Children and Family Futures

Adriana Garza
Mayfair Improvement
Initiatives

R. Charles Gatson
Community Builders of
Kansas City

James Gibson
Center for the Study of
Social Policy

Elwood Hopkins
Los Angeles Urban Funders

Craig Howard
Manpower Demonstration
Research Corporation

Sandy Jibrell
The Annie E. Casey
Foundation

Earl Johnson
California Health and
Human Services Agency

Grantland Johnson
California Health and
Human Services Agency

Otis Johnson
Savannah State University

Doris Koo
Seattle Housing Authority

Sally Leiderman
Center for Assessment and
Policy Development

May Louie
Dudley Street Neighborhood
Initiative

Elisabethe Mack
Detroit Neighborhood
Family Initiatives

Joseph McNeely
The Development Training
Institute

Anita Miller
Comprehensive Community
Revitalization Program

Maurice Lim Miller
Asian Neighborhood Design

William A. Morrill
Caliber Associates

Kristen Moy
The Aspen Institute

Mary Nelson
Bethel New Life

Sandy O'Donnell
Center for New Horizons

Robert J. O'Neill, Jr.
National Academy of Public
Administration

Alvertha Bratton Penny
The William and Flora
Hewlett Foundation

Beverly Perkins
Memphis Orange Mound
Collaborative

Terry Peterson
Resource Network for
Afterschool and
Community Education

Edward Phelan
Highbridge Community
Life Center

Patricia Press
Marshal Heights Community
Development Organization

Sheila Radford-Hill
Bethel New Life

Ronald Register
Consultant

Charles Ridley
The Village Foundation

Irma E. Rodriguez
The Forest Hills Community
House

Ann Segal
The David and Lucile
Packard Foundation

Miriam Shark
The Annie E. Casey
Foundation

Ralph Smith
The Annie E. Casey
Foundation

Cris Stainbrook
Indian Land Tenure
Foundation

Jay Allen Stokes
Inner City Redevelopment
Corporation

Cornelia Swinson
Germantown Settlement

Allan M. Tibbels
Sandtown Habitat for
Humanity

Susan Tibbels
New Song Community
Learning Center

Julie Thomasson
    MDC, Inc.

Avis Vidal
    Wayne State University

Alice Wadsworth
    Wadsworth and Associates

Michael Wald
    The William and Flora
        Hewlett Foundation

Vanessa White
    North East Milwaukee
        Industrial Development
        Corporation

Gayle Williams
    Mary Reynolds Babcock
        Foundation

Junious Williams
    Urban Strategies Council

APPENDIX III

FOR FURTHER READING

Overview and Historical Context

Briggs, Xavier de Souza. 2002. *Community Building: The New (and Old) Politics of Urban Problem-Solving.* Boston: Harvard University.

Bruner, Charles, and Larry Parachini. 1997. *Building Community: Exploring New Relationships across Service Systems Reform, Community Organizing, and Community Economic Development.* Washington, D.C.: Institute for Educational Leadership.

Chaskin, Robert J., Mark L. Joseph, and Selma Chipenda-Dansokho. 1997. "Implementing Comprehensive Community Development: Possibilities and Limitations." *Social Work* 42(5): 435–43.

Dodson, D., and J. Thomasson. 1997. *Building Communities of Conscience and Conviction: Lessons from Recent Experience.* Chapel Hill, N.C.: MDC.

Edelman, Peter. 2001. *Searching for America's Heart: RFK and the Renewal of Hope.* New York: Houghton Mifflin.

Ferguson, Ronald F., and William T. Dickens, eds. 1998. *Urban Problems and Community Development*. Washington, D.C.: Brookings Institution.

Ferguson, Ronald F., and Sara E. Stoutland. 1998. "Community Development, Change and Sustainability in Community Support Systems." In *Urban Problems and Community Development*, ed. Ronald F. Ferguson and William T. Dickens. Washington, D.C.: Brookings Institution.

Fulbright-Anderson, Karen, and Patricia Auspos, eds. Forthcoming. *Community Change: Theories, Practice, and Evidence*. Washington, D.C.: Aspen Institute.

Grogan, Paul S., and Tony Proscio. 2000. *Comeback Cities: A Blueprint for Urban Neighborhood Revival*. Boulder, Colo.: Westview Press.

Halpern, Robert. 1995. *Rebuilding the Inner City: A History of Neighborhood Initiatives to Address Poverty in the United States*. New York: Columbia University Press.

Jackson, Maria-Rosario, and Peter Marris. 1996. *Collaborative Comprehensive Community Initiatives: Overview of an Emerging Community Improvement Orientation*. Washington, D.C.: Urban Institute.

Jargowsky, Paul A. 1997. *Poverty and Place: Ghettos, Barrios, and the American City*. New York: Russell Sage Foundation.

Kingsley, Thomas G., Joseph McNeely, and James O. Gibson. 1997. *Community Building: Coming of Age*. Washington, D.C.: Urban Institute.

Kubisch, Anne C., Prudence Brown, Robert Chaskin, Janice Hirota, Mark Joseph, Harold Richman, and Michelle Roberts. 1997. *Voices from the Field: Learning from Comprehensive Community Initiatives*. Washington, D.C.: Aspen Institute.

Kubisch, Anne C., Carol H. Weiss, Lisbeth B. Schorr, and James P. Connell. 1995. "Introduction." In *New Approaches to Evaluating Community Initiatives: Concepts, Methods, and Contexts*, ed. James P. Connell et al. Washington, D.C.: Aspen Institute.

Leiterman, M., and J. Stillman. 1993. *Building Community.* New York: Local Initiatives Support Corporation.

Marris, Peter, and Martin Rein. 1973. *Dilemmas of Social Reform: Poverty and Community Action in the United States.* Chicago: Aldive.

Mattessich, Paul W., and Barbara R. Monsey. 1997. *Community Building: What Makes It Work, A Review of Factors Influencing Successful Community Building.* St. Paul, Minn.: Amherst H. Wilder Foundation.

Mollenkopf, John H. 1983. *The Contested City.* Princeton, N.J.: Princeton University Press.

Nyden, Philip, Anne Figert, Mark Shibley, and Darryl Burrows. 1997. *Building Community: Social Science in Action.* Thousand Oaks, Calif.: Pine Forge Press.

O'Connor, Alice. 1999. "Swimming against the Tide: A Brief History of Federal Policy in Poor Communities." In *Urban Problems and Community Development,* ed. Ronald F. Ferguson and William T. Dickens. Washington, D.C.: Brookings Institution.

———. 2001. *Poverty Knowledge: Social Science, Social Policy, and the Poor in Twentieth-Century U.S. History.* Princeton, N.J.: Princeton University Press.

Pierson, John, and Joan Smith. 2001. *Rebuilding Community: Policy and Practice in Urban Regeneration.* New York: Palgrave.

Pitcoff, Winton. 1997. "Redefining Community Development." *Shelterforce* 19(6): 2–14.

Stone, Rebecca. 1996. *Core Issues in Comprehensive Community-Building Initiatives.* Chicago: Chapin Hall Center for Children at the University of Chicago.

Vidal, Avis C. 1992. *Rebuilding Communities: A National Study of Urban Community Development Corporations.* New York: Community Development Research Center, Graduate School of Management and Urban Policy, New School for Social Research.

Walsh, Joan. 1996. *Stories of Renewal: Community Building and the Future of Urban America.* New York: Rockefeller Foundation.

Wilson, William Julius. 1987. *The Truly Disadvantaged: The Inner City, the Underclass and Public Policy.* Chicago: University of Chicago Press.

Zielenbach, Sean. 2000. *The Art of Revitalization: Improving Conditions in Distressed Inner-City Neighborhoods.* New York: Garland.

Comprehensive Community Initiatives: Descriptions and Evaluations

Brown, Prudence, B. Butler, and R. Hamilton. 2001. *The Sandtown-Winchester Neighborhood Transformation Initiative: Lessons Learned about Community Building and Implementation.* Baltimore: Annie E. Casey Foundation.

Brown, Prudence, and Paul S. Stetzer Jr. 1998. *Glades Community Development Corporation: A Chronicle of a Community Development Intermediary.* Chicago: Chapin Hall Center for Children at the University of Chicago.

Burns, Thomas, and Gertrude Spilka. 1997. *The Planning Phase of the Rebuilding Communities Initiative.* Philadelphia: OMG Center for Collaborative Learning.

————. 1998. *The Planning Phase of the Rebuilding Communities Initiative: Technical Assessment Report.* Philadelphia: OMG Center for Collaborative Learning.

Annie E. Casey Foundation. 1995. *The Path of Most Resistance: Reflections on Lessons Learned from New Futures.* Baltimore: Annie E. Casey Foundation.

Center for the Study of Social Policy. 1995. *Building New Futures for At-Risk Youth: Findings from a Five-Year, Multi-Site Evaluation.* Washington, D.C.: Center for the Study of Social Policy.

Chaskin, Robert J. 2000. *Lessons Learned from the Implementation of the Neighborhood and Family Initiative: A Summary of Findings.* Chicago: Chapin Hall Center for Children at the University of Chicago.

Chaskin, Robert J., Selma Chipenda-Dansokho, and Mark L. Joseph. 1997. *The Ford Foundation's Neighborhood and Family Initiative: The Challenge of Sustainability.* Chicago: Chapin Hall Center for Children at the University of Chicago.

Chaskin, Robert J., Selma Chipenda-Dansokho, and C. J. Richards. 1999. *The Ford Foundation's Neighborhood and Family Initiative: Entering the Final Phase*. Chicago: Chapin Hall Center for Children at the University of Chicago.

Chaskin, Robert J., Selma Chipenda-Dansokho, and Amanda K. Toler. 2000. *Moving beyond the Neighborhood and Family Initiative: The Final Phase and Lessons Learned*. Chicago: Chapin Hall Center for Children at the University of Chicago.

Chaskin, Robert J., and Mark L. Joseph. 1995. *The Ford Foundation's Neighborhood and Family Initiative: Moving toward Implementation*. Chicago: Chapin Hall Center for Children at the University of Chicago.

Chaskin, Robert J., and R. Ogletree. 1993. *The Ford Foundation's Neighborhood and Family Initiative: Building Collaboration*. Chicago: Chapin Hall Center for Children at the University of Chicago.

Conservation Company. 1995. *Sandtown-Winchester Community Building in Partnership 1990–1994*. Philadelphia: Conservation Company.

Cornerstone Consulting Group. 1998. *Communities in the Balance: Reflections on the Neighborhood Preservation Initiative*. Albany, N.Y.: Nelson A. Rockefeller Institute of Government, Urban and Metropolitan Studies, State University of New York.

Cutler, Ira. 1997. *Learning Together: Reflections on The Atlanta Project*. Atlanta: Carter Center.

EZ/EC Foundation Consortium, and Community Development Associates, Inc. Forthcoming, 2002. "Voices from the Empowerment Zones: Insights about Launching Large-Scale Community Revitalization Initiatives." Baltimore: Annie E. Casey Foundation.

Giles, Michael. 1994. *Evaluation of the Atlanta Project, Part 1: Plan and Implementation*. Atlanta: Carter Collaboration Center.

———. 1995a. *Evaluation of the Atlanta Project, Part 2: Analysis and Findings*. Atlanta: Carter Collaboration Center.

———. 1995b. *Evaluation of the Atlanta Project, Phase II: Interim Report*. Atlanta: Carter Collaboration Center.

Leviten-Reid, Eric. 2001. *Opportunities 2000: Multisectoral Collaboration for Poverty Reduction: Final Evaluation Report.* Ottawa: Caledon Institute of Social Policy.

Local Initiatives Support Corporation. 1996. *Community Building Initiative: Chicago, Detroit, Indianapolis, Kansas City, Los Angeles, Miami, New York, Philadelphia, Phoenix, St. Paul, Washington, D.C.* New York: Local Initiatives Support Corporation.

Los Angeles Urban Funders. 2001. *A Project of the Southern California Association for Philanthropy: Five-Year Summative Report, 2001.* Los Angeles: Southern California Association for Philanthropy.

Milligan, S., M. Nario-Redman, and C. Coulton. 1997. The *1995–1996 Cleveland Community-Building Initiative Baseline Progress Report.* Cleveland: Center on Urban Poverty and Social Change, Mandel School of Applied Social Sciences, Case Western Reserve University.

Milligan, S. E., M. Nario-Redman, and J. Norton. 1999. *The 1997–1998 Cleveland Community-Building Initiative Baseline Report on Collaborative Relationships.* Cleveland: Center on Urban Poverty and Social Change, Mandel School of Applied Social Sciences, Case Western Reserve University.

Naperstek, Arthur J., Susan R. Freis, and G. Thomas Kingsley. 2000. *Hope VI: Community Building Makes a Difference.* Washington, D.C.: U.S. Department of Housing and Urban Development.

Nelson A. Rockefeller Institute of Government. 1996. *An Assessment of the Empowerment Zone/Enterprise Community Initiative.* Albany, N.Y.: Nelson A. Rockefeller Institute of Government, Urban and Metropolitan Studies, State University of New York.

Price Waterhouse. 1997. *Empowerment Zone Initiative, Activities for Strategic Change: An Overview of Public and Private Investment Activities in the Six Urban Empowerment Zones.* Arlington, Va.: Price Waterhouse.

Riccio, James A. 1999. *Mobilizing Public Housing Communities for Work: Origins and Early Accomplishments of the Jobs-Plus Demonstration.* New York: Manpower Demonstration Research Corporation.

Spilka, Gertrude, and T. Burns. 1994. *First Annual Assessment Report: Comprehensive Community Revitalization Program.* Philadelphia: OMG Center for Collaborative Learning.

———. 1998. *Final Assessment Report: The Comprehensive Community Revitalization Program in the South Bronx.* Philadelphia: OMG Center for Collaborative Learning.

Sviridoff, M., and W. Ryan. 1996. *Investing in Community: Lessons and Implications of the Comprehensive Community Revitalization Program.* New York: Comprehensive Community Revitalization Program.

Walsh, Joan. n.d. *The Eye of the Storm: Ten Years on the Front Lines of New Futures.* Baltimore: Annie E. Casey Foundation.

Wright, D. J., and J. G. Carman. 1996. *Neighborhoods That Work: An Assessment of the Pew Charitable Trusts' Neighborhood Preservation Initiative.* Albany, N.Y.: Nelson A. Rockefeller Institute of Government, Urban and Metropolitan Studies, State University of New York.

Foundations and Funding

Brown, Prudence, Robert Chaskin, Ralph Hamilton, and Harold Richman. 2002. "Toward Greater Effectiveness in Community Change: Challenges and Responses for Philanthropy." Chicago: Chapin Hall Center for Children at the University of Chicago. Working draft.

Brown, Prudence, and Sunil Garg. 1997. *Foundations and Comprehensive Community Initiatives: The Challenges of Partnership.* Chicago: Chapin Hall Center for Children at the University of Chicago.

Cohen, Rick. 2000–2001. "Community Action and Responsive Philanthropy: A Natural Partnership." *Community Action Digest* 2(2): 27–32.

Collins, Dennis A. n.d. *The Art of Philanthropy: Personal Reflections on the Craft.* San Francisco: James Irvine Foundation.

Cutler, Ira. 2002. *End Games: The Challenge of Sustainability.* Baltimore: Annie E. Casey Foundation.

David, Tom. 2000. "Reflections on Strategic Grantmaking." *The California Wellness Foundation, Reflections Series* 2 (November).

Hamilton, Ralph. 2002. *Moving Ideas and Money: Issues in Funder Collaboration.* Chicago: Chapin Center for Children at the University of Chicago.

Hearn, Ruby. 2001. "Interview." *Advances: The Robert Wood Johnson Foundation Quarterly Newsletter* 2:4.

Neighborhood Effects and Social Capital

Booth, A., and A. C. Crouter, eds. 2001. *Does It Take a Village? Community Effects on Children, Adolescents, and Families.* Mahwah, N.J.: Erlbaum.

Briggs, Xavier de Souza, Elizabeth J. Mueller, and Mercer L. Sullivan. 1997. *From Neighborhood to Community: Evidence on the Social Effects of Community Development.* New York: Community Development Research Center, Robert J. Milano Graduate School of Management and Urban Policy, New School for Social Research.

Brooks-Gunn, Jeanne, Greg J. Duncan, and J. Lawrence Aber, eds. 1997a. *Neighborhood Poverty, Volume 1: Context and Consequences for Children.* New York: Russell Sage Foundation.

———. 1997b. *Neighborhood Poverty, Volume 2: Policy Implications in Studying Neighborhoods.* New York: Russell Sage Foundation.

Brown, Prudence, and Kitty Barnes. 2001. *Connecting Neighbors: The Role of Settlement Houses in Building Social Bonds within Communities.* New York: Chapin Hall Center for Children at the University of Chicago and United Neighborhood Houses in New York.

Chaskin, Robert J. 2001. *The Evaluation of Community Building: Measuring the Social Effects of Community-Based Practice.* Chicago: Chapin Hall Center for Children at the University of Chicago.

Coleman, J. S. 1988. "Social Capital in the Creation of Human Capital." *American Journal of Sociology* 94 (Summer): 95–120.

DeFilippis, James. 2001. "The Myth of Social Capital in Community Development." *Housing Policy Debate* 12(4): 781–806.

Foley, M. W., and B. Edwards. 1997. "Escape from Politics? Social Theory and the Social Capital Debate." *American Behavioral Scientist* 40(5): 550–61.

Furstenberg, Frank, T. D. Cook, J. Eccles, G. H. Elder Jr., and A. Samaroth. 1999. *Managing to Make It: Urban Families and Adolescent Success.* Chicago: University of Chicago Press.

Furstenberg, Frank, and M. Hughes. 1995. "Social Capital and Successful Development among At-Risk Young." *Journal of Marriage and Family* 57 (August): 580–92.

Potapchuk, W., W. Schecter, J. Crocker, C. Benero, and M. Bailey. 1999. *Communities That Work: Exploring the Elements of Civic Capital.* Washington, D.C.: Program for Community Problem Solving Publications, division of the National Civic League.

Putnam, Robert D. 1993. "The Prosperous Community: Social Capital and Public Life." *American Prospect* 13: 1–8.

———. 1995. "Bowling Alone: America's Declining Social Capital." *Journal of Democracy* 6(1): 65–78.

———. 2000. *Bowling Alone: The Collapse and Revival of American Community.* New York: Simon and Schuster.

Saegert, Susan, and Gary Winkel. 1998. "Social Capital and the Revitalization of New York City's Distressed Inner-City Housing." *Housing Policy Debate* 9(1): 17–60.

Saegert, S., M. R. Warren, and J. P. Thompson, eds. 2001. *Social Capital and Poor Communities.* New York: Russell Sage Foundation.

Saguaro Seminar. 2001. "Social Capital Community Benchmark Survey: Executive Summary." In *The Saguaro Seminar: Civic Engagement in America.* Boston: John F. Kennedy School of Government, Harvard University.

Temkin, Kenneth, and William M. Rohe. 1998. "Social Capital and Neighborhood Stability: An Empirical Investigation." *Housing Policy Debate* 9(1): 61–88.

Woolcock, M. 1998. "Social Capital and Economic Development: Toward a Theoretical Synthesis and Policy Framework." *Theory and Society* 27: 151–208.

Evaluation, Research, and Learning

Bruner, Charles, Mark Greenberg, Cynthia Guy, Michael Little, Lisbeth Schorr, and Heather Weiss. n.d. *Funding What Works: Exploring the Role of Research on Effective Programs and Practices in Government Decision-Making.* Des Moines: National Center for Service Integration and Clearinghouse and the Center for Schools and Communities.

Chavis, David, Kien Lee, and Elizabeth Jones. 2001. *Principles for Evaluating Comprehensive Community Initiatives.* Gaithersburg, Md.: Association for the Study and Development of Community.

Clements, P., A. Turner, K. Bailey, and M. Pagni. 1999. *Success Measures Guide Book.* Boston: Development Leadership Network.

Connell, James P., Anne C. Kubisch, Lisbeth B. Schorr, and Carol H. Weiss, eds. 1995. *New Approaches to Evaluating Community Initiatives: Concepts, Methods, and Contexts.* Washington, D.C.: Aspen Institute.

Fulbright-Anderson, Karen, Anne C. Kubisch, and James P. Connell, eds. 1998. *New Approaches to Evaluating Community Initiatives, Volume 2: Theory, Measurement, and Analysis.* Washington, D.C.: Aspen Institute.

Kingsley, Thomas G., ed. 1999. *Building and Operating Neighborhood Indicator Systems: National Neighborhood Indicators Partnership Report.* Washington, D.C.: Urban Institute.

Moore, K. S., S. Rees, M. Grieve, and D. Knight. 2001. "Program Evaluation in Community Development." In *Working Paper Series.* Washington, D.C.: Aspen Institute Nonprofit Sector Research Fund.

Pauly, Edward. 2001. "Common Sense and Assessment." Presentation for NYRAG Spring 2001 Program, *Learning from Our Experience: Assessing the Work of Grantmakers.* New York: DeWitt Wallace-Reader's Digest Fund and Lila Wallace-Reader's Digest Fund.

Rossi, Peter H. 1999. "Evaluating Community Development Programs: Problems and Prospects." In *Urban Problems and Community Development*, ed. Ronald F. Ferguson and William T. Dickens. Washington, D.C.: Brookings Institution.

Torjman, Sherri, Eric Leviten-Reid, Christopher Camp, and Anne Makhoul. 2001. *From Information to Application: How Communities Learn*. Ottawa: Caledon Institute of Social Policy.

Wandersman, Abe, Dana Keener, Jessica Snell-Johns, Paul Flaspohler, Melanie Dye, and Julia Mendez. 2002. *Principles of Empowerment Evaluation*. Columbia: University of South Carolina Press.

Capacity Building

Backer, T. E. 2000. *Strengthening Nonprofits: Capacity-Building and Philanthropy*. Miami: Knight Foundation.

Brown, Prudence, Jessica Pitt, and Janice Hirota. 2000. "New Approaches to Technical Assistance: The Role of the Coach." *Community: A Journal of Community Building for Community Leaders* 3: 20–27.

Campobasso, Laura, and Dan Davis. 2001. "Reflections on Capacity Building." *The California Wellness Foundation, Reflection Series* 2 (April).

Chaskin, Robert J., Prudence Brown, Sudhir Venkatesh, and Avis Vidal. 2001. *Building Community Capacity*. New York: Aldine de Gruyter.

Conservation Company. n.d. *Building to Last: A Grantmaker's Guide to Strengthening Nonprofit Organizations*. Philadelphia: Conservation Company.

Development Training Institute. 2000. *Competency Study of Leaders Who Facilitate Successful Community Building Initiatives*. Baltimore: Development Training Institute.

Glickman, Norman J., and Lisa J. Servon. 1998. "More Than Bricks: Five Components of Community Development Corporation Capacity." *Housing Policy Debate* 9(3): 497–539.

Ewing Marion Kauffman Foundation. 2001. *Profiles in Organizational Effectiveness for Nonprofits: Improving the Lives of Children, Youth and Families in Kansas City.* Kansas City, Mo.: Ewing Marion Kauffman Foundation.

Light, Paul C. 2002. *Pathways to Nonprofit Excellence.* Washington, D.C.: Brookings Institution.

Light, Paul C., and Elizabeth T. Hubbard. 2002. *The Capacity Building Challenge.* Washington, D.C.: Brookings Institution.

Nye, Nancy. n.d. *Sustainable Strength: An Interim Report of the Capacity Building Program Evaluation.* New York: Corporation for Supportive Housing.

Nye, Nancy, and Norman J. Glickman. 2000. "Working Together: Building Capacity for Community Development." *Housing Policy Debate* 11(1): 163–98.

Governance and Collaboration

Bardach, Eugene. 1998. *Getting Agencies to Work Together: The Practice and Theory of Managerial Craftsmanship.* Washington, D.C.: Brookings Institution.

Brown, Prudence, Jessica Pitt, and Janice Hirota. 1999. *Collaborative Approaches to Revitalizing Communities: A Review of the Neighborhood Strategies Project.* Chicago: Chapin Hall Center for Children at the University of Chicago.

Chaskin, Robert. n.d. *Fostering Neighborhood Democracy: Foundations, Local Government, Community Organizations, and the Issue of Neighborhood-Based Governance.* Chicago: Chapin Hall Center for Children at the University of Chicago.

Chaskin, Robert, and Clark Peters. 2000. *Decision Making and Action at the Neighborhood Level: An Exploration of Mechanisms and Processes.* Chicago: Chapin Hall Center for Children at the University of Chicago.

Kato, Linda Y., and James A. Riccio. 2001. *Building New Partnerships for Employment: Collaboration among Agencies and Public Housing Residents in the Jobs-Plus Demonstration.* New York: Manpower Demonstration Research Corporation.

Pitcoff, Winton. 1998. "Redefining Community Development, Part II: Collaborating for Change." *Shelterforce* 19(1): 2–17.

Resident Participation and Community Organizing

Applied Research Center. 2000. *Grassroots Innovative Policy Program.* Oakland, Calif.: Applied Research Center.

Gitell, Marilyn et al. 1998. *Empowerment Zone Implementation: Community Participation and Community Capacity, 2nd Year Report.* New York: Howard Samuels State Management and Policy Center, Graduate School, and University Center of the City University of New York.

Gittell, Ross, and Avis Vidal. 1998. *Community Organizing: Building Social Capital as a Development Strategy.* Thousand Oaks, Calif.: Sage.

Hertz, Judy. n.d. *Organizing for Change: Stories of Success.* Skokie, Ill.: Desktop Edit Shop.

Parachini, Larry, and Sally Covington. 2001. *Community Organizing Toolbox.* Washington D.C.: Neighborhood Funders Group.

Walker, Karen E., Bernardine H. Watson, and Linda Z. Jucovy. 1999. *Resident Involvement in Community Change: The Experiences of Two Initiatives.* Philadelphia: Public/Private Ventures.

Community Connections to External Resources

Briggs, Xavier de Souza. 2002. *The Will and the Way: Local Partnerships, Political Strategy and the Well-Being of America's Children and Youth.* Cambridge, Mass.: Harvard University Press.

Bruner, Charles, Martin Blank, and the Together We Can Partnership. 2000. *Human Service Systems Reform: Lessons from the Rebuilding Communities Initiative on the Challenges for Disinvested Neighborhoods and the Challenges for Systems.* Des Moines: Child and Family Policy Center.

Gardner, Sid. 2001. *Cities, Counties, and Kids: The Critical Role of Local Governments in Children's Policy.* Fullerton: California State University, Fullerton.

Granovetter, Mark S. 1973. "The Strength of Weak Ties." *American Journal of Sociology* 78(6): 1360–80.

International Institute for Environment and Development. 2002. "Globalization and Cities." *Environment & Urbanization* 14(1).

Katz, Bruce, ed. 2000. *Reflections on Regionalism*. Washington, D.C.: Brookings Institution.

Martin, Roger L. 2002. "The Virtue Matrix: Calculating the Return on Corporate Responsibility." *Harvard Business Review* 80(3): 68–75.

Moy, Kirsten, and Alan Okagaki. 2002. "Changing Capital Markets and Their Implications for Community Development Finance." *Neighborhood Funders Group* 1(9).

Pastor, Manuel, and Peter Dreier, Eugene Grigsby III, and Marta Lopez-Garza. 2000. *Regions That Work: How Cities and Suburbs Can Grow Together*. Minneapolis: University of Minnesota Press.

PolicyLink. 2000. *Perspectives on Regionalism: Opportunities for Community Based Organizations to Advance Equity*. Oakland, Calif.: PolicyLink.

Porter, Michael. 1995. "The Competitive Advantage of the Inner City." *Harvard Business Review* 73(3): 55–71.

Saasta, Tim. 2001. *Getting Ahead: New Approaches to Generating Jobs and Opportunities for Residents of Low Income Communities*. Washington, D.C.: Center for Community Change.

Race and Ethnicity

Blackwell, Angela, Stewart Kwoh, and Manuel Pastor. 2002. *Searching for the Uncommon Common Ground: New Dimensions on Race in America*. New York: American Assembly.

Chang, Hedy Nai-Lin. 1997. *Community Building and Diversity: Principles for Action*. Oakland, Calif.: California Tomorrow.

Chang, Hedy Nai-Lin, Louie Nguyen, Ben Murdock, Elena Pell, and Ted Scott Femenella. 2000. *Walking the Walk: Principles for Building Community Capacity for Equity and Diversity*. Oakland, Calif.: California Tomorrow.

Institute for Democratic Renewal and Project Change Anti-Racism Initiative. n.d. *A Community Builder's Tool Kit:15 Tools for Creating Healthy, Productive Interracial/Multicultural Communities*. Claremont, Calif.: Claremont Graduate University.

Lawrence, Keith O. 2001. "Race and Community Revitalization." New York: Aspen Institute. Draft report.

Massey, Douglas S., and Nancy A. Denton. 1993. *American Apartheid: Segregation and the Making of the Underclass.* Cambridge, Mass.: Harvard University Press.

Potapchuk, Maggie. 2001. *Steps toward an Inclusive Community.* Washington, D.C.: Joint Center for Political and Economic Studies.

powell, john. 1998. "Race and Space: What Really Drives Metropolitan Growth." *Brookings Review* (Fall).

————. 2000. "Addressing Regional Dilemmas for Minority Communities." In *Reflections on Regionalism,* ed. Bruce Katz. Washington, D.C.: Brookings Institution.

Stone, Rebecca, and Benjamin Butler. 2000. *Core Issues in Comprehensive Community-Building Initiatives: Exploring Power and Race.* Chicago: Chapin Hall Center for Children at the University of Chicago.